WHEN
THE WAR
ENDS

WHEN THE WAR ENDS

STUART CHASE has been commissioned by the Trustees of The Twentieth Century Fund to make a series of exploratory reports on postwar problems. These are being published under the general title, "When The War Ends," and the books are planned to appear at intervals of a few months during 1942 and 1943. The present volume explores basic issues and fundamental trends. Later books in the series will examine specific questions of postwar readjustment. The tentative list of titles follows:

1

The Road We Are Traveling: 1914-1942

2

Goals for America: A Budget of Our Needs and Resources

3

The Dollar Dilemma: Problems of Postwar Finance

4

Tomorrow's Trade: Problems of Our Foreign Commerce

5

Farmer, Worker, Businessman: Their Place in Postwar America

6

Winning the Peace

THE ROAD
WE ARE
TRAVELING
1914-1942

Guide lines to America's future

as reported to

THE TWENTIETH CENTURY FUND

by

STUART CHASE

NEW YORK

THE TWENTIETH CENTURY FUND

1942

MANUFACTURED IN THE UNITED STATES OF AMERICA

FOREWORD

AMERICA IS AT WAR. The first objective of all of us must be to win.

Once we look to the end of the war, however, we see a task hardly less gigantic than victory itself. This is the task of turning our economy back to peacetime uses.

Clearly, the very sinew of our war effort will be affected by the goals we see ahead. Planning for peace has become second only in importance to winning the war.

The Trustees of the Twentieth Century Fund foresaw this need even before Japanese treachery at Pearl Harbor on December 7, 1941 pushed us into the war itself. The armies that overran France in June 1940 trampled down our last chance of maintaining a normal peacetime economy. From the first defense appropriations of that beleaguered summer, through the Lend-Lease Act of March 1941 to the present time, ours has been a steadily mounting effort to prepare for the eventuality of war. The Fund Trustees, early in 1941, decided to do what they could to help plan for the inevitable aftermath— the day when we should have to demobilize our war economy and return to peacetime pursuits.

Defeatism about the peace is almost as dangerous as defeatism about the war. The victory need not and must not lead to economic depression and disaster at home. Actually, when peace does come, it will be an opportunity and a challenge: an opportunity to use our vastly increased plant and human resources to raise the standard of living for us all; a challenge to make a greater civilization.

The purpose of this book—and several more which are to follow—is to lay out, as clearly as can be done, what the economic problems of the peace are likely to be.[1]

Nor can we look at these problems in a vacuum. The United States is fighting in a world war, and inevitably we must play our part in making a world peace. The contribution we can make will be largely determined by conditions in our country and what we can do to solve our own problems. It is essential that we understand these as a basis for any consideration of our role in a world order.

The situation being new, the Trustees of the Fund decided to adopt a new policy to meet it. Normally, in dealing with peacetime problems, the Fund sets up a special research staff to make a careful, factual investigation; and appoints a nonpartisan committee of qualified persons to review the findings and use them as a basis for recommendations as to public policy. But, by definition, trying to preview the future is radically different from attempting to solve a concrete problem in the present. Here, past performances are primarily important as contrasts with today and tomorrow.

The first task in dealing with the future is to try to foresee its outlines and contours. This calls for bold, imaginative

1. A recent pamphlet published by the Fund, which will be periodically revised and reissued, describes the research planned or under way in the field of United States postwar reconstruction by other agencies. George B. Galloway, *Postwar Planning in the United States*.

thinking: for prevision rather than research. To get this thinking into use, lucid, vigorous writing is essential.

The Fund has asked Stuart Chase to tackle this formidable
assignment. It has made available to him the facilities of the
Fund and consultation with the Fund's staff in planning the
project and preparing manuscript. It has provided him with
the assistance of Mr. A. B. Handler in assembling factual
material and has arranged conferences with various well-
informed persons whose views might be of value. Through it
all, however, the Fund has left Stuart Chase completely free
to reach his own conclusions.

This book is a sort of taking-off point for others in the
series. It is easier to see where we are going if we get a clear
picture of the road we have traveled and its general direction.
I believe this first example of the Fund's method of approach-
ing postwar problems amply warrants the entire undertaking.
Mr. Chase's conclusions, of course, are his own, and are not
necessarily those of the Twentieth Century Fund. But the
Fund Trustees believe that Mr. Chase's explorations offer perhaps the best available method of crystallizing thought about
events which will determine the lives of all of us before many
years have passed.

In presenting this first volume in the series, "When the
War Ends," I am glad to express the appreciation of the
Trustees to Mr. Chase for undertaking this assignment; and
to Evans Clark, the Fund's Director, and Dr. J. Frederic Dew-
hurst, its Economist, for their assistance in planning the project and their help to Mr. Chase in carrying it out.

A. A. BERLE, JR.

WASHINGTON, D. C.
MARCH 3, 1942

AUTHOR'S PREFACE

THE STUDY of which this book is the first installment was begun some months before the Japanese attack on Pearl Harbor. Since then many people have asked me, "Why think about postwar problems now? We have not won the war yet!" The best answer that I can give is to advise the questioner to go along Main Street as if he were taking a sidewalk opinion poll and ask every person he meets if postwar problems are important. He will find, I think, that every American is in this war and is determined to win. But there is hardly a conscious American who is not wondering right now about what is likely to happen to his home, his job, his world, when the war ends.

I believe, moreover, that we are more likely to win the war if we have a clear idea of goals for the peace. Men fight better when they know for what they are fighting. Any peace we make must be superior to that which our enemies can offer. They make alluring promises about new orders and new spheres of prosperity. These promises are widely heard in the lands most affected, and we shall have to do more than sneer at them. We shall have to—and can—offer something better, more just and more convincing.

The United States may come out of this war the strongest nation on earth. To be worthy of that strength, we should take the lead in plans for permanent co-operation among our allies; in plans for permanent co-operation among the peoples of the whole world if that be possible. We must be careful not to repeat the tragic mistakes of the Treaty of Versailles.

In concentrating my main attention on the United States in this series I am carrying out the wishes of the Trustees of The Twentieth Century Fund. To do so does not imply that our postwar policies should not harmonize with those of other nations. Already in our own hemisphere the policies of the twenty-one republics are closely interlocked. But any agenda must have an order, and the primary position should go to one's own country. Our task will begin, even if it does not end, at home.

STUART CHASE

CONTENTS

8 *Contents*

THE ROAD WE ARE TRAVELING
1914-1942

1

PATTERN OF CHANGE
1914—1942

THE UNITED STATES along with the rest of the world is in deep trouble today. Some people think it all started with Hitler, others that it started when the Japanese invaded Manchuria, others when the stock market fell apart, when the Treaty of Versailles was signed. These events have undoubtedly helped the trouble along, but we must not forget that history is a seamless process, in which many causes produce many effects, which are in turn causes for more effects, world without end.

If Haber in Germany had not perfected the process of tearing nitrogen out of the air when he did, thus making the Reich independent of imports of nitrates from Chile, the first World War would not have started when it did. Maybe it would not have started at all. Things do not happen suddenly, out of nowhere. There is always a long and often complicated chain of reasons. In this book I propose to try to discover some of the reasons which have landed us where we are. If the story makes it plain that the present has flowed out of the past without interference by inexplicable devils, we may perhaps feel less helpless about the future. We are riding a curve which began many years ago.

THE "NEW FREEDOM," 1913-1914

Let us take a stroll down State Street in Boston in the Spring of 1913. The tulips are up in the Public Gardens, the boys are playing baseball on the Common, and Woodrow Wilson has just been inaugurated President of the United States. The First National Bank is not dreaming of merging with anybody. Lee Higginson and Company, in its quaint corner on a cobbled lane, is as near to Heaven as any young man recently graduated from Harvard College is likely to aspire. Mr. Wilson with his New Freedom is proposing some dubious legislation and he has that fellow Bryan in his cabinet, but bonds are sound, stocks are climbing and 6 per cent is as orthodox as the Ten Commandments. Out West they are getting 8 per cent and more. It is an orderly universe. There are a few wall-sided automobiles along the curbs, no neon lights, no radios, no organized super-salesmen.

Since Napoleon was defeated at Waterloo a century ago, there have been no great world wars. During this century the population of the Western World has trebled, that of the United States has increased twelvefold. When the century began, the work of Western civilization was done by the muscles of men, horses, oxen, assisted by a few leaky, thumping steam engines. When the century ended, the work was done by inanimate energy from coal, oil, falling water, assisted by the muscles of men. Horses and oxen were already suffering the pangs of technological unemployment.

During the century, the United States pushed its boundaries to the Pacific and closed the frontier, while the Great Powers of Europe completed the division of Africa, Asia and Australasia. By 1913, there were no more free lands in the United States, and no more free territories left to colonize except

Antarctica. Captain Scott had just died of the cold there, after his immortal march to the South Pole. It was a century of such expansion as the world had never seen before, and will probably never see again.

Why Change?

As we walk through the crooked streets of Boston, still filled with horse-drawn vans, we do not realize that behind us lies the most abnormal century in economic history. We look at the solid banks, the solid buildings, the solid merchants and the solid dray horses, and expect everything to go right on. It has been a good century, on the whole—prosperous, enterprising, dynamic; why should it not go right on? Mr. Wilson with his New Freedom has inaugurated the income tax, the Federal Reserve Board and the Federal Trade Commission, but after all, Mr. Wilson is a disciple of John Stuart Mill—and who could be sounder than that?—and perhaps a few legislative reforms are necessary. At any rate Teddy Roosevelt, with his socialistic Bull Moose party, has been eliminated. If you can believe it, he was actually in favor of votes for women. Everyone knows what that means: the destruction of the home, the church, and the American form of government. Did Washington advocate votes for women; did Jefferson? Wilson is also tinkering with the tariff. The tariff should no more be tinkered with than should the gold standard. Hard money and protection are what have made this country great. Mr. Bryan can initial peace treaties to his heart's content as Secretary of State, so long as he drops his nonsense of 16 to 1. Government, as everybody knows, is not a respectable business anyway. Few young men from Harvard dream of entering government service. The rightful place of government is to act as umpire, and keep out of competition with honest businessmen.

The philosophy of laissez-faire is the accepted creed of all right-thinking persons. The fact that trusts have been formed in meat packing, steel, anthracite coal, farm machinery, paper manufacturing, is regrettable in principle, but as practical men along State Street we know that competition can be carried to unreasonable limits. That anarchist, Debs, and his friends make plenty of noise, but what have they to show for it? Nothing but a few municipal waterworks. Socialism will never make headway in this country. Why, if you divided up all the money. . . . The trade unions are weak, the farmers are self-supporting, independent, and can never be organized, the I.W.W. will not get anywhere except with bums who have forgotten how to work. Brandeis can rant about the Money Trust in *Other People's Money,* but everybody in Boston knows what Brandeis is. Upton Sinclair can stir up class hatred by writing *The Jungle,* but Sinclair is a radical and not to be trusted. With a million immigrants coming in a year, it is important that subversive doctrines be kept down.

Almost thirty years later, a British professor summarized the situation on State Street in 1913, and on Wall Street and Threadneedle Street as well:

Enterprising individuals could solve the economic problem by migration, enterprising nations by colonization. Expanding markets produced an expanding population, and population in turn reacted on markets. Those who were left behind in the race could plausibly be regarded as unfit. A harmony of interests among the fit, based on individual enterprise and free competition, was sufficiently near to reality to form a sound basis for current [economic] theory. With some difficulty the illusion was kept alive until 1914.[1]

1. E. H. Carr, *The Twenty Years' Crisis, 1919-1939.*

All Is Well?

The British navy is supreme on the seas. The pound sterling is supreme on the world's markets. Trade routes are open to all comers, and the gold standard is almost universal. The British have 20 billions of foreign investments, Americans but 3 billions. The United States is a debtor nation, owing more abroad than is owed to it. All young men along State Street read Kipling, and most of them agree as to the soundness of the "white man's burden." President McKinley inaugurated dollar diplomacy with the Spanish War, and now we are carrying the white man's burden in Cuba, Porto Rico and the Philippines. The Germans are talking about Berlin to Bagdad, the British are talking about Cape to Cairo, the Russians are talking about Constantinople and a warm water port.

The peace of Europe is maintained by a delicate balance of power. Britain, France and Russia in the Triple Entente face Germany, Austria and Italy in the Triple Alliance. The "stout little Japs" have recently whipped the Russians in Manchuria. Some Americans acclaim their "fight for freedom" and others foresee a Yellow Peril to the United States. Parliamentary democracy is at an all-time high, the world around. Even the Russians now have a Duma. Mr. Lloyd George has struck a great blow for democracy in Britain by threatening to pack the House of Lords with double the number of peers, in a fight about the budget. The Lords capitulated and all power now belongs to the Commons.

Britannia rules the waves, but Germany, France, the United States, Belgium, Japan, are pushing hard against her industrial supremacy. The United States and Germany have indeed surpassed her industrial output. Nations that once were "backward" are beginning to build factories of their own. The trade of the world is nominally free but Britain alone of the Great Powers is not protected by tariffs.

War is a business for professional soldiers, and foreign affairs a business for professional diplomats. The people are not interested. Secret treaties? Why, of course. The Czar has inaugurated the Hague Tribunal for arbitrating international disputes. Again, the people are not interested.

A new cult is abroad in America, and even businessmen in State Street are talking about it. Started by Frederick W. Taylor, it is called "scientific management," and all members of the cult are busy time-studying themselves, stop watch in hand. Is this motion unnecessary? Eliminate it, and save money. Another industrial engineer, Walter Polakov, has set up a mechanism to run a power plant by remote control, without a man in the place. A mechanic named Henry Ford is putting motor cars into mass production. In 1910, the number of people working on farms in the country began to decline, though crop production continued to increase. Scientific methods are coming into agriculture. The number of patents issued is soaring. Science and invention show no signs of slackening. The economy of scarcity, where population presses on production, is almost over. Production is getting out in front. This is a condition never known before.

Turning Points

One of the most important things happening on this spring morning will not be revealed until many years later. Some time after the turn of the century, the growth rate of many American industries, after bounding upward for decade after decade, began to decline. Such a time had to come. Dr. Raymond Pearl points out, for instance, that if the production of coal had continued to grow at the rate it was growing in the 1890's "it would not be long before it would reach a produced tonnage such that the entire globe would have to be of solid coal to permit of its realization."[2] Yet businessmen and bankers have been taught by the phenomenal expansion of the nineteenth century to believe that: "the continuation of such constant growth is our concept of normality in business." Despite the huge immigration, even the growth rate of population is beginning to decline.

All seems to be well with the world on this spring morning, but below the surface history is getting ready for some momentous changes. The formulas which served the enterprising and the fit so well for over a hundred years and more are wearing thin, and in fifteen months all hell will break loose in Europe, presently to engulf the United States.

THE WAR TO END ALL WARS, 1914-1919

When the World War began in 1914, it was a matter of scurrying diplomats, professional soldiers in control, and business as usual. When it ended in 1918 it was a matter of "total" war, with most civilians involved in some patriotic capacity, and governments, run by virtual dictators, in almost complete control of the economic and cultural life of the nation. Toward the close of the struggle, the Supreme Economic Council of the Allies, with headquarters in London, was rationing the raw materials of half the world.

This was the first scientific war on the planet. The machine gun made killing a mass production process. Ten million men

2. Quoted by Bassett Jones in *Debt and Production,* page 33.

were killed in battle or died of wounds; twenty million civilians were killed by war-borne disease; and the cost was estimated at 186 billion dollars—a figure to give even New Dealers pause. Airplanes, poison gas, submarines, tanks, machine guns, all made their first appearance in a big way. Propaganda, assisted by telephone, cable, wireless, high-speed presses and Four Minute Men, was recognized as almost as important as guns.

Out of propaganda techniques, designed to confound the enemy and bolster the faithful, was to come much of the high-pressure advertising of the 1920's. Out of the new mechanical and industrial techniques designed to speed the output of ships and shells, was to come the magnificent mass production plant of the United States and Germany. Out of wartime collectivism was to come a permanent and growing invasion of private business by the state. Out of the war control of shipping, raw materials and foreign trade were to come economic nationalism and the disintegration of the world free market.

State Street in 1923 looked much like State Street in 1913, except for the rash of brass-appointed motor cars—but the old certainties had been undermined. In the Spring of 1933, with the doors of the First National Bank closed and Lee Higginson and Company gasping for air, they were dead. Young men from Harvard, young men from anywhere, knew not which way to turn. The rhythm of the nineteenth century was missing a beat or two, for those with ears to hear, before the war began. The war finished it quite finally. Men had now to find other assumptions upon which to base their economic lives. Most of them did not know it in the early 1920's. Many do not know it yet.

In August 1914, when crowds in the streets of Paris were singing the Marseillaise and shouting "On to Berlin!" crowds in the streets of Boston, New York, Chicago, were looking for work. A serious depression was gathering. It continued for some months while the German armies overran Belgium, surged toward Paris, were driven back at the Marne, and finally dug in behind a line of trenches which ran from the mud of Flanders to the Alps. British and French purchasing agents came over to the United States to buy mountains of munitions and food. J. P. Morgan and Co. took charge of the financial arrangements. Orders were placed, men were called off the streets to go to work and fill them. Farmers began to expand their acreage for wheat, even out into the dry farming areas of the Great Plains. By the middle of 1915, a war boom had overwhelmed the depression. It continued to grow and roar, up to 1920. Prices, wages, rents, land values, went up with employment, and presently the high cost of living was on every housewife's tongue. Many businessmen made huge profits throughout the period, though after the United States entered the war, taxes recaptured a large part of them.

War Crosses the Ocean

Mr. Wilson's New Freedom was soon forgotten in the excitement of war abroad. The President had his hands full in trying to maintain the doctrine of the freedom of the seas against both British seizures of American ships and the German submarine blockade, and in trying to pacify, with American guns, a revolutionary Mexico.

The *Lusitania* went down with more than one hundred Americans aboard. The bankers refused to finance Allied purchases any longer, thus threatening the jobs of millions of

munitions workers and farmers. The Germans resumed unre-
stricted submarine warfare, and Wilson led a somewhat unwilling country into war. The government underwrote the
bankers' loans to the Allies. Farmers and munitions workers
were made busier than ever, with American war purchases
added to those of France, Britain and Italy.

War was declared in April 1917, and for a time economic
chaos reigned. Conscription had been voted. Five million
young men were to be withdrawn from their jobs and if necessary delivered overseas, together with fifty times their
weight of steel, artillery, barbed wire, wheat, tin cans and
TNT. They could not swim. Ships had to be borrowed or
built. As the war began, the army, the navy, the purchasing
agents of the Allies, and domestic buyers in a panic at the
thought of rising prices, all descended on the market and
screamed for billions of dollars' worth of goods to be delivered instantly.[3]

To make matters worse, 90 per cent of the orders were placed
in the northeast corner of the country, until freight cars were
dumping their loads in open fields thirty miles from term-
inals. Factories were depleted of skilled workers by the draft,
while orders mounted to the skies. Copper shot from 15 cents
a pound to 37 cents. Speculators, shoestring operators, fixers,
swarmed amid the turmoil, cornering essential products. The
railroad system, with each company trying to keep the cream
of the traffic on its own lines, had broken down.

The Birth of "Planning"

If this planlessness continued, not only would no soldiers
be moved to France, but the civilian population would starve

3. See Grosvenor B. Clarkson, *Industrial America in the World War*.

to death waiting for freight cars which lay helpless in traffic jams. The government did the only thing possible. It took over the railroad system of the country and appointed William G. McAdoo as Administrator. He allowed no competitive nonsense. He moved freight on the nearest available rails, no matter who owned them. With the cooperation of the War Industries Board, which was headed by Bernard Baruch, the knots in traffic and in orders were gradually unravelled.

The War Industries Board in due course became the central planning agency for the whole American economy. It had no particular legal authority, but what were laws at a time like this? The Board stopped the industrial pandemonium with clearance orders. It started a steady flow of goods with priority orders. It correlated the requirements of the army, the navy, the Allies and the domestic market. Observe the latter came last. It inventoried industrial plants to determine how, where and when their requirements could be met. It expanded facilities to meet them, closed up nonessential production, crippled the output of luxury goods, made patents and secret processes common property if they stimulated production anywhere, set up regional controls to prevent one section of the country from becoming over-congested or over-prosperous. It forced great technical improvements through simplification and standardization of products, reallocated skilled and unskilled labor, and forecast, if you please, almost the exact day of the Armistice, by virtue of its study of raw material depletion in Germany. No plants were taken over, but if a given concern did not cooperate, a word to the Fuel Administration cut off its coal supply, and a word to Mr. McAdoo cut off its freight cars.

New Highs for Production

What the War Industries Board really did was to make it possible to lift one third of the productive man power of the country into the army and munitions services, and to keep the remaining population fully and purposefully employed at a somewhat higher standard of living than it had ever before enjoyed.[4] In brief, the Board so organized the national economy that two men did the work of three, and did it better. Old gentlemen in the bay windows of clubs began to complain bitterly about silk shirts on boilermakers. The lag, leak and friction of business as usual was dramatically demonstrated. Given the psychological drive—in this case, war and patriotism—it was clear that a planned economy was capable of staggering increases in output with an actual decline in man power. The lesson lay there for all to see. The economy of abundance was swinging into focus.

By 1918, the total war pattern was luminous in all belligerent countries. Every available civilian was at work. National income, government debt, taxes, were enormously increased. Prices were fixed by decree, vital supplies rationed, labor conscripted, capital allocated, production directed not to the market but to specific war ends, profits heavily taxed, crosshauling eliminated, foreign trade monopolized by the government. In five great Liberty Loan drives, the United States raised 21 billion dollars—"give until it hurts"—and passed on 11 billions in loans to twenty foreign countries without security. Most of it, with accumulated interest, is still on the cuff. When the war ended, we found ourselves a creditor nation for the first time in our history. We found ourselves, indeed, the strongest industrial and financial nation on earth.

4. See computations in the author's *The Tragedy of Waste,* page 5.

Business concerns were allowed to charge advertising and research outlays to cost before figuring their profits. Wartime taxes on these profits were very high. Many concerns thought it advisable to keep their money at home by enlarging their advertising and research departments—especially after the Armistice. The result was a great subsidy for those high-pressure selling methods which characterized the 1920's, and are not unknown today, and another great subsidy for industrial research, scientific management and mass production.

The A. O. Smith Corporation of Milwaukee began to build the first large automatic factory in the world. In this plant automobile frames were made almost entirely by inanimate energy and machines. Many more automatic plants were to follow. War, and the taking over of German patents, stimulated a whole new chemical industry in the United States. The war also stimulated the labor movement.

On the battlefronts of Europe, glory and gallantry almost left the field in this first great struggle of machines. There was no general subsequently to be christened the Great, like Napoleon and Frederick. It was a war of fabulous supply trains moving to the front, there to produce horizontal sheets of lead and steel projectiles. The human nervous system was stretched to its breaking point. The airmen, in their bamboo crates, were said to have enjoyed the war but nobody else did. Back and forth the lines swayed on the Western Front for more than four bloody, muddy, terrible years. All the world's factories worked night and day so that a mile of churned earth might be gained here and a salient closed there. The whole European economy was distorted, as peasants left their farms for the trenches and workers specialized on war supplies.

The Crisis of Peace

President Wilson's Fourteen Points helped to break the deadlock. The Germans, with their armies intact but their supply lines failing, grasped at the Fourteen Points as a way out. On November 11, 1918 the Armistice was signed, and the world went mad with joy. The war to end war was over. But it turned out that it was only an armistice after all. Twenty years later the guns were roaring again. The treaty of Versailles, the League of Nations, the elaborate machinery set up to make peace permanent, were not strong enough to hold the line.

The war wiped out three great dynasties—the Hapsburgs, the Hohenzollerns and the Romanoffs, but there was the usual amount of political dynamite left in Europe. Russia went communist, Germany, after a short civil war, went republican, and the Empire of the Hapsburgs went every which way. Fifty million soldiers and war workers were demobilized in an economic system undone by ruined fields, blasted cities, wrecked factories and mountains of paper debts. The debts were presently wiped out or scaled down by inflation or devaluation. They had to be, for they made no sense if Europeans were to work and eat again.

Mr. Hoover went over to feed starving people. Dr. Nansen took charge of the terrible problem of refugees. Socialism, communism, unrest and revolution were in the air. In belligerent and neutral countries all over the world, factory output and crops had been artificially stimulated by war orders. After the war, each nation struggled to maintain its expanded output. "An enhanced and inflamed national consciousness," says Professor Carr, "was invoked to justify the struggle." This was one reason for what he calls the "unprecedented vindictiveness" of the peace treaties. Practical men no longer believed in the "harmony of interest" theory of international trade. They tried rather to eliminate competitors, a revival of whose prosperity might menace their own. Germany was crushed under a 33 billion dollar indemnity.

Anyone who studies the economic history of the war carefully should not be surprised at the subsequent appearance of Mussolini, Hitler, Stalin, national socialism, barter deals, communism, autarchy, the new order in Asia, the New Deal in America, the economic disintegration of the British Empire. They were all on the cards by 1920. A dreadful war had been followed by a dreadful treaty of peace, and nothing had been settled. It was too late to go back to the formulas of 1913, and only the Marxists had a plan for going forward. Their plan was grim, idealistic and impracticable, as subsequent events in Russia proved.

Consider the idols which the war had smashed:[5]

Free enterprise within nations was replaced by planned economies, government controlled.

Free speech was replaced by censorship and propaganda.

Free world markets were replaced by government control of exports and imports, by subsidies, blockades, and the sinking of 20 million tons of merchant ships with their cargoes.

The gold standard was abandoned.

The whole credit structure was wiped out in some countries, distorted in all, while relationships between debtors and creditors were shattered by inflation and devaluation.

The old doctrine of the freedom of the seas was found to be unworkable in the face of fleets of submarines. (In the face of long-range bombers, it is even more so.)

5. Some returned to an uneasy status in the 1920's.

Britannia still ruled the waves, but the economic solidity and prosperity of the British Empire had been dealt a serious blow. It ceased to be the paying proposition it had been in the nineteenth century. The financial center of the world shifted from London to New York. The wonder men of Wall Street did not know what to do with it.

"Normalcy," 1920-1929

When the several delegates came home from the peace conference in Paris, they hoped that they had arranged matters so that the world could return to normal competitive business within nations, normal trade between nations. Everyone was sick and tired of war and wanted a sane world again. The logical definition of sanity was the condition before 1914. In only one country was the hope even partially realized—the United States. President Harding called it "normalcy," a strange word to cover a strange condition.

After the postwar boomlet had spent its energy, America fell into a steep depression, with 6 million unemployed, in 1921. Then we climbed out and went floating away on one of the most curious eras of prosperity which the world had ever seen. It brought us to an all-time peak in 1929 and then we joined other nations in abnormal depression and despair, and abnormal attempts to keep from going under altogether.

In post-war Europe, planned economy, which rests on the assumption that no natural harmony of interests exists, and that interests must be harmonized by state action, became the practice, if not the theory, of every state. In the United States, the persistence of an expanding domestic market staved off this development until after 1929.[6]

6. E. H. Carr.

Why did we prosper, while other countries remained flat on their backs, with only occasional attempts to sit up and take notice? Britain, for instance, struggled back to the gold standard in 1926, but after five years of desperate hanging on, fell off again. We prospered, I believe, because we were not hurt by the war as much as the other nations. We still had expanding markets. We were not so dependent on foreign trade as were they, and we had a wonderful new toy to play with—the automobile. It made four million new jobs and absorbed vast quantities of steel, copper, glass, lumber, aluminum, petroleum and concrete. It was a device particularly adapted to American continental distances, with no passports to show every few miles, and to American mass production methods. The United States has been called an experiment in transportation. The motor car fitted this experiment, as the railroads had fitted it earlier, and the rivers and canals earlier still.

Bases of "Prosperity"

There were other reasons for prosperity. During the war we neglected building houses, and after the war the shortage was made good. We also had a fine time building skyscrapers, first in Manhattan and then in the middle of theTexas prairies. We had a fine time converting the swamps and keys of Florida into elegant properties valued at $1,000 a front foot. We had a fine time running up installment credit to the 6 billion dollar mark. All the way up it increased spending power and aided prosperity. We had a particularly fine time—or our bankers did—investing some 10 billions of our capital abroad. We helped to rebuild German industry, construct Polish harbors, Peruvian highways, Yugoslavian mines, and what have you.

This kept our workers busy supplying the goods which foreigners ordered with the proceeds of our loans. It gave other countries brief shots of prosperity. It enriched a lot of fixers, and gave the bankers good commissions. It made everybody happy while it lasted. There was only one regrettable feature: most American investors were subsequently cleaned out.

To sum up, American "normalcy" was built on an active construction industry—which began to taper off in 1928; on the automobile industry—which reached a replacement market toward the end of the decade; on installment credit increases—which had an ultimate ceiling; on foreign loans— which went very sour before the decade was over; on the stock market boom—which with stocks selling in no tangible relation to their earning power, made less and less sense as the decade wore on.

For the seven years from 1922 to the world collapse of 1929, the national income went up; employment remained at high levels; wages were relatively good; trade unions lost ground, while jazz bands and flaming youth made enormous headway; station KDKA in Pittsburgh sent the returns of the 1920 elections over the air, and the radio industry was born; farmers as a class were in the red together with the textile, soft coal and shoe industries; Americans began to write first-class novels and pretty good poetry; most prices did not increase, which is an unheard-of thing in a boom; Ford changed over from Model T to Model A and precipitated a minor depression while tooling up; Harding, Coolidge and Hoover kept government out of business with an almost theological zeal, but government spending and taxes per capita went steadily up; federal debts declined but local government debts increased, due to servicing skyscraper cities, roads and schools; everybody complained about prohibition but nobody did anything about it; the cult of "service" was born, and businessmen in conference became the lords of creation; investment trusts became fashionable along Wall Street; immigration was throttled way down, and the birth rate, after 1925, began to fall heavily; a boy named Lindbergh flew across the ocean to France and the nation went wild with joy; women's skirts went above their knees, summer and winter, day and night, and furnished one of the reasons for the chronic indisposition of the textile trades. (It is interesting to note that skirts came down with the stock market in the fall of 1929.) In brief, it was a wonderful seven fat years, but normal was hardly the term to apply to it.

Cracks in the Underpinning

Free enterprise was the toast of all trade association banquets, but two harsh forces were hammering away at the traditional free markets. They were not so obvious as the state controls practiced during the war, but they were strong. One was the pressure of technology, the other was the steady growth of "administered" prices in industry.

In 1920 the number of workers in manufacturing, mining and railroading reached a peak—as the number of workers in agriculture had reached a peak in 1910—and began to decline. Output from the factories and mines increased during the decade, but the number of workers went down. This meant that output per man-hour was going up, which meant that the inventors, research laboratories and industrial engineers were hard at work. Staggering gains in efficiency were made in many industries. The machine age, with its dingy coal and iron base, began to give way to the power age, with its electric motor, high-power transmission and aluminum base. The photoelectric cell began to take over skilled jobs of measuring, weighing, inspecting. Conveyor systems, semi-automatic and full automatic factories were introduced. The sweating toiler retreated before the skilled inspector and dial watcher.

To drill four holes in a number of metal plates so that they bear a fixed relation to the edges of the plates, requires a skilled craftsman to operate the ordinary drilling machine. But if a jig is devised whereby the plates can be secured by setscrews, the drill can come down to a thousandth of an inch every time. A robot can do the job. If, however, the number of plates to be drilled is large, a new type of machine can be installed which will perform the task automatically, twenty-four hours a day, with nobody in attendance except an occasional inspector. Both skill and thought have been replaced by the machine. Human thought leaves production and concentrates on the design of the mechanism. Then you throw a switch and Niagara Falls, or Harlan County coal, does the work. Production became no trick at all, and mental effort flowed over into the selling end.

What happened to the workers displaced in manufacturing, mining and railroading? They went, many of them, into the service trades. A machinist who lost his job to an automatic press might borrow some money and open a garage. If you want a quick and vivid picture of the growing service trades, take a look along U. S. Route 1. Dr. Wesley C. Mitchell estimated in 1927 that some 650,000 workers displaced from the primary industries never did connect with a garage, a filling station or a dry-cleaning outfit. They joined the ranks of the permanent army of the unemployed. Throughout the period, technological unemployment was a growing menace, speeding up the displacement rate even if the net figure for unemployment did not much increase. "Firing at forty" also became common in this era of prosperity.

For every 100 persons engaged in manufacturing in 1919, there were 94 in 1929. Output per person was estimated to have increased 53 per cent. For every 100 working on the railroads in 1920 there were only 84 in 1929. The number of farmers dropped from 6,387,000 in 1920 to 6,012,000 in 1930; coal miners from 759,000 to 646,000; lumbermen from 195,000 to 159,000. But during the same period, wholesale and retail trade personnel shot up from 4,215,000 to 6,094,-000; clerks from 1,540,000 to 2,102,000; professional people from 2,203,000 to 3,110,000.[7]

The "Competition" of Giants

Throughout the terms of Harding, Coolidge and Hoover, corporations grew bigger, mergers became more frequent, holding company pyramids got closer and closer to the trackless voids of interstellar space. By 1930, according to Berle and Means, some 200 mammoth corporations accounted for about half of all industrial activity. They did not play the game according to the rules of free competition. They were not exactly "trusts" in the 1913 sense, but they in effect fixed prices. They competed mildly with one another but within a price range limited by themselves. "The shift from free market to administered prices," says Dr. Means, "is the development which has destroyed the effective functioning of the American economy and produced the pressures which culminated in the new economic agencies of the government." Wal-

7. Figures from *Recent Social Trends*.

ter Lippmann phrased it thus: "In a realistic view of the old capitalism, it is not far from the truth to say that free competition existed in so far as men were unable to abolish it."

Mass production had been greatly advanced by the war. To set up a plant for mass-produced goods requires a large amount of capital. When the plant is built it can often supply a very considerable fraction of the national need. A few such plants can service the whole national market. Thus a condition is created, primarily by reason of the technology of quantity production, where free competition, in the Adam Smith sense of small plants with a high death rate, is unworkable. "Monopoly" is not quite the word for it, as one group is not always in control. A new and ugly word, taken from the Greek, has been coined for the situation—"oligopoly," meaning "few sellers." The automobile industry is a good example, where General Motors, Ford and Chrysler account for the bulk of the cars manufactured. Even with no intention to control prices, a market in which three or four sellers produce most of the output is necessarily controlled. Adam Smith's free competition works only when sellers are so numerous and so small that the prices fixed by any one of them do not affect the market for the others in any fundamental way. The market price is practically independent of the actions of any one seller. That is the condition to which the term "free competition" refers. It was a condition that no longer obtained over great areas of American industry.

Not only giant corporations "administered" their markets, but little concerns got together in trade associations and did the same so far as they were able. If a member cut prices according to the canons of supply and demand, he was called a "chiseler," and became a moral outcast. Labor unions, when they could contrive it, did precisely the same thing. They declared a closed shop and defied the free market with rigid wage rates. Thus, while foreign nations were abandoning the free market formula for international cartels and experiments in government controls, the United States, nominally the citadel of private enterprise, was moving to a similar end by a different route.

Meanwhile a curious shift had occurred in corporate control. Stockholders continued to own the property, but came to have less and less voice in the management. A new class of self-perpetuating managers, controlling policy by various legal devices, was swinging into power. The stockholder had the promise of a conventional dividend if he was a good boy, and a proxy which he could throw in the wastebasket.

Overseas, President Wilson's principles of self-determination for small nations were not working well. The facts of technology and a high energy economy demanded large geographical units over which railroads, power lines, the flow of goods, could run without the interruption of customs barriers, armed frontiers and separate currencies. The United States was so organized, but Europe was not. The Treaty of Versailles, rather than helping the situation, made it worse. The old Austrian, Russian, Turkish and German empires were carved into eight shiny new nations, with customs houses, ambassadors and standing armies all complete. The new sovereign states included Finland, Poland, Estonia, Latvia, Lithuania, Czechoslovakia, Yugoslavia, Hungary, while Austria was hacked down to a little territory around the city of Vienna—all head and no body. They were democracies on paper, but all except Czechoslovakia were presently ruled by dictators. Cultural minorities within the new states seethed with unrest, especially in Poland, Yugoslavia and Czechoslovakia. "The liberal democracies scattered throughout the world by the peace settlement of 1919," says Professor Carr, "were the product of abstract theory, struck no roots in the soil, and quickly shrivelled away."

Fruits of U. S. Isolation

The League of Nations struck no roots in the soil, either. It had no armed force behind it. Neither Britain nor France was ready to delegate any part of its national sovereignty to the League. Without such delegation, and the armed power which goes with it, no league of nations can do much more than get out reports on how to check the hoof and mouth disease. The League at Geneva published many admirable reports and arbitrated a few minor quarrels; but when the real tests came in Manchukuo, Ethiopia and Spain, it was helpless.

The failure of the United States to join the League brought Wilson to his grave. If we had joined it, would we have surrendered our sovereignty any more than did Britain or France? Would we have allowed the League to modify the Monroe Doctrine, for instance? The world had gone ahead too far to tolerate eight new nations in a Europe which called for the economic unity of the Continent. It had not gone ahead far enough to accept a real League, with real battleships and bombers to enforce its decisions. A League without bombers is only a debating society. When a powerful member wants to annex some real estate from a weaker member, he resigns and mobilizes his troops. The debaters say tut! tut! and declare the meeting adjourned. The League of Nations could do nothing for Haile Selassie but pass resolutions. British guns and tanks gave him back his Empire.

Mussolini marched on Rome in 1923 and set up the corporate state, where government rigorously controlled business and workers. Russia destroyed the free market altogether and replaced it with complete state control and the first Five Year Plan of 1928. Sweden developed an interesting "mixed" economy, where government ownership and regulation, giant cooperative associations, and private business shared the field, with political democracy still strongly functioning. Australia and New Zealand pushed ahead with social legislation, spurred by strong labor parties. Britain boosted income taxes and turned the proceeds into doles, subsidized housing and social welfare, while her classic policy of free trade became more and more untenable as backward nations took her trade away. Horrible blighted areas, where industry had once hummed, appeared in the British Isles.[8]

Prelude to Collapse

When Germany defaulted on her preposterous 33 billion dollar war indemnity, the French army marched into the Ruhr. Riots and bloodshed followed. The Germans refused to work or pay taxes. The mark fell precipitously. The famous inflation of 1923 followed—a very special case, as you can see—which ended with 518 quintillion paper marks in circulation. To buy a cabbage you needed a bushel basket full of money. The creditor class was wiped out, but businessmen, relieved of their debts and aided by American loans, proceeded to "rationalize" German industry on the basis of the latest power age techniques. Great cartels were set up to control production. They were nominally owned by tycoons like Krupp and Thyssen, but the depression of 1929 soon made

8. See J. B. Priestley's *English Journey*.

them inoperable under private management, and they fell, dead ripe, into the basket of national socialism.[9]

Dictators seized power in Poland, Spain, Greece, Turkey, Yugoslavia—all over the place. Every nation, including the United States with its stupendous tariff wall, tried to become more self-sufficient, to sell more than it bought, to protect its economy with trade barriers, export subsidies, preferential agreements, "Buy British" campaigns. Markets closed by the war and blockade had not reopened on the old pattern. The United States had swung from a debtor to a creditor nation, and then attempted the curious task of boosting its tariffs so that it could export more than it could import. This mathematical impossibility collapsed in 1928, when investors stopped tossing American dollars abroad. In another year the whole economic structure collapsed, both here and abroad. Why should it not? It was tied together with safety pins and old string. The mass of the people had been sick of the war in 1918. They were now getting sick of a safety-pin economy which gave them no security and very little hope.

THE DEPRESSION TO END ALL DEPRESSIONS, 1930-1939

The big gong had hardly sounded in the great hall of the Exchange at ten o'clock Tuesday morning before the storm broke in full force. Huge blocks of stock were thrown upon the market for what they would bring. Five thousand shares, ten thousand shares appeared at a time on the laboring ticker at fearful recessions in price. Not only were innumerable small traders being sold out, but big ones too, protagonists of the new economic era who a few weeks before had counted themselves millionaires. Again and again the specialist in a stock would find himself surrounded by brokers fighting to sell—and nobody at all even thinking of buying. . . .

9. See Robert A. Brady, *The Rationalization of German Industry*.

Despite the jamming of the communication system, orders to buy and sell—mostly to sell—came in faster than human beings could possibly handle them. . . . Within half an hour of the opening the volume of trading had passed 3,000,000 shares, by twelve o'clock it had passed 12,000,000, and when the closing gong brought the day's madness to an end the gigantic record of 16,410,030 shares had been set. The average prices of 50 leading stocks, as compiled by *The New York Times,* had fallen nearly 40 points. Meanwhile there was near-panic in other markets—the foreign stock exchanges, the lesser American exchanges, the grain market.

Thus Frederick Lewis Allen in *Only Yesterday* (published by Harper) immortalized the day when normalcy fell apart, and the prophets of the "new era" in American business with no more depressions and two cars in every garage, were confounded. They did not know what had hit them, and did not believe it for months.

On October 25, 1929 just before Terrible Tuesday, the 29th, President Hoover made a statement to the Press: "The fundamental business of the country is on a sound and prosperous basis." On March 8, 1930, a Washington dispatch read: "President Hoover predicted today that the worst effect of the crash upon unemployment will have passed during the next 60 days." On January 1, 1930 the Secretary of the Treasury, Andrew W. Mellon, in a New Year's message reported: "I see nothing in the present situation that is either menacing or warrants pessimism." Arthur Brisbane in his syndicated column assured the nation: "All the really important millionaires are planning to continue prosperity." He was right. The important millionaires were planning to continue prosperity but they might as well have been planning to make the Mississippi River run north.[10]

10. For a hilarious list of erroneous prophecies during this period, see *Oh Yeah?,* compiled by Edward Angley.

In Sunnyside Gardens on Long Island in 1929, 500 families were living happily and prosperously in a model suburban community. They were mostly professional people, writers, artists, architects, businessmen. An inventory of their situation as a group was made in 1932, three years after the big gong sounded. Their combined income had been cut in half. Their income from investments had been reduced to negligibility. Two families out of five had one or more members unemployed. Half of all life insurance policies had been cancelled, while loans on remaining policies had cut the equity in half. Bank deposits had been depleted by 76 per cent. All assets had been depleted by 78 per cent compared with 1929. Half the group could no longer retain their homes in Sunnyside without financial help. Unpaid doctor and dentist bills had increased 150 per cent. Personal borrowings had increased 578 per cent. In brief, this group of intelligent, hard-working professional citizens was sunk. Citizens in the lower income group were in a worse fix financially, but as they were more used to crises, their mental torture was presumably not so great. This was the first American depression to hit the middle classes a solar plexus blow, and even reach up and tumble many important millionaires into the gutter. Nobody was immune. All over the nation, great estates with thirty-room mansions and ten master bathrooms became a drug on the market.

Roots of the Depression

Did the crash in Wall Street bring on the depression? No. Wall Street only dramatized a condition which lay deeper.

Let us go back to that spring morning on State Street in 1913. By that time, the American frontier had closed, the rates of population and production growth were levelling off. All the world had been pretty well divided up by the Great Powers, with colonial development slackening. Backward nations were beginning to build their own factories. In 1914 a depression came. It might have been a serious depression but we pulled out of it on war orders and spending for armaments, until every able-bodied man was in the army or employed. After the war, we fell into another depression. We pulled out of that on deferred construction, foreign loans, installment credit and the giant motor car and highway investment. Other nations were not so fortunate. They remained mostly in a trough of permanent depression.

What is a business depression? For one thing, it is a period where the rate of investment in capital goods slows down. Savings, instead of being invested, gather in stagnant pools. Idle money in monetary systems always breeds idle men. As we noted earlier, all the major outlets for investment in job-making enterprises began to decline toward the end of the twenties. People had built nearly all the houses they could afford; businessmen were complaining about excess capacity.[11] The Brookings Institution, after a careful study of the situation in 1929, found an excess capacity which averaged 20 per cent for the nation. If one has all the machines he needs and then some, why buy more? The volume of installment credit had reached a temporary ceiling, and prospects for realizing on foreign loans looked worse and worse.

As a nation we had been saving about 20 per cent of the national income during the period, according to Dr. Lauchlin Currie's testimony before the TNEC. These savings began to

11. For instance, the Wool Institute complained in 1927 that the excess capacity of the industry was 200 per cent.

back up. The savings-investment mechanism is the flywheel of a capitalistic economy. The news leaked into Wall Street— a little cloud the size of a man's hand. Market quotations were higher than any reasonable hope of future earnings would permit. This made all operators who were not quite mad a bit uneasy, too. The cloud spread, and spread—and then the big gong sounded.

Dr. Alvin H. Hansen of Harvard, in summarizing the period, says that there can be little question that the boom in investment during the twenties, followed by saturation in investment outlets and the decline in the output of fixed capital goods, was "the central core of the great world depression, and determined mainly its intensity and duration."[12] Observe that the depression was not due to government interference. Businessmen, keeping cool with Coolidge and hot with Hoover, had a relatively free hand. The unions were quiet. The socialists had declined to a political pinpoint. The radicals were reading H. L. Mencken or writing advertising copy.

Tail Spin

Down, down, down. Unemployment grew from an estimated 2 million in 1929 to 15 million in 1933, nearly a third of the whole labor force of the country. National income dropped from 80 billion dollars to 40 billions; the value of manufactured products from 70 billions to 31 billions. In 1932, corporations as a group were 6 billions in the red, and 68,000 industrial concerns dropped into limbo. At one time, the construction industry was operating at less than 20 per cent of its 1929 volume, and for five years it made no profits at all. By 1934, 45,000 miles of railway lines were in receiver-

12. See his *Fiscal Policy and Business Cycles*.

ship. The sale of durable goods fell to a third of its 1929 level, and foreign trade was off 65 per cent. The cash income of all farmers was 13 billions in 1920, 11 billions in 1929, 5 billions in 1932. Wheat was selling at 32 cents a bushel, cotton at 6 cents a pound, beef at $3.20 a hundredweight. Wheat on the Liverpool market fetched the lowest price since the reign of Charles II.

Was this a bottomless pit? Economists following business cycle theory said that things which go down, must come up. Economists, bank presidents, politicians, Mr. Charles M. Schwab, Mr. Richard C. Whitney, after their cheery peeks around the corner in 1930, were silent, their stock in the sub-basement along with Radio Common. This was a depression which only God could see the end of.

There came a time when Mr. Hoover could not let nature take its course in continued deflation. More than 6,000 banks had failed since 1928. Farmers were threatening to hang sheriffs who foreclosed their neighbor's homesteads. Boy and girl hoboes were on the roads by the tens of thousands. People were eating garbage in the Chicago dumps, shack slums were springing up on the outskirts of every town, the wretched Bonus Army was marching on Washington. Mr. Hoover threw aside his principles of laissez faire, and inaugurated an embryo new deal. He expanded public works, put relief on a federal basis through grants to the states, and organized the Reconstruction Finance Corporation to put government credit under tottering railroads, insurance campanies and banks. He was forced to unbalance the budget, and so became the unwilling parent of deficit spending, two years before Mr. Roosevelt became a patron. No better illustration could be given to show that the depression was stronger than politics, stronger than economic theories. Statesmen had to bend to the wind.

It was not enough. The banking situation rushed to a dreadful climax at a rate which approximated geometrical progression. The Detroit banks folded, then Michigan, then two states, four states, blocks of states, until banks in 32 states had locked their doors on the day Mr. Hoover left office. This was the gravest day the United States of America had ever seen.

Mr. Roosevelt stood in the rain, taking the oath of office on the steps of the Capitol, and asked for "broad executive power to wage a war against the emergency, as great as the power that would be given to me if we were invaded by a foreign power." He quieted a terrified nation with his first fireside chat. Congress gave him the power for which he had asked. During the next 100 days he promulgated one law after another which had the effect of stopping deflation, and then reversing the down-trend into a dizzy little up-trend in commodity prices and the stock market. In 1937 there was another sharp drop, but we never again scraped the 1933 bottom. The national income staggered back, with government assistance, to 70 billion dollars.

New Deal to the Rescue

The New Deal went into action on all fronts—financial, agricultural, industrial, and just plain human. It was welcomed deliriously. The NRA parade in New York recalled the reception to Lindbergh. But the honeymoon of national unity did not last for long. Nothing in the agenda of the New Deal was as radical as the war agenda of 1917 in respect to the government control of economic activity. But it was far beyond anything ever attempted in peace time. By 1935, with the organization of the Liberty League, the opposition became very bitter indeed. It was partly traditional Republican hostility to Democrats, but even more it was horror at the violation of traditional ideas about what the government should and should not do. People were hungry, people were losing their homes, farmers were sullen, 10 or 12 million industrial workers were still on the streets, business concerns were losing vast sums of money because of the shrinkage in purchasing power. The New Deal went on. It had to; either something like it or back to the yawning gulf of 1933.

The federal government was receiver for a bankrupt economy. History will record it so. The economy was bankrupt not only in a flow of goods inadequate to keep millions of its people above the line of destitution, bankrupt in the utter collapse of business leadership, but bankrupt technically. The whole banking system was insolvent in 1933; liabilities exceeded assets at current valuations. Whatever the economic structure was which had brought a great nation to this pass, it was not good enough. Its moral beauties, if it had moral beauties, could no longer offset the tragic fact of people beaten to their knees, workless and starving in a land of material plenty. A structure which better fitted the necessities of survival in the power age had to be found, and the New Deal was the first attempt to find it.

As the depression deepened, the woods were full of plans and schemes to improve or revolutionize the structure—Technocracy, EPIC, Social Credit, Social Justice, the Utopians, the Townsend Plan, self-help communities using token money, Huey Long's remarkable program to make every man a king. The alphabetical agencies of the New Deal acted while the schemers talked, and the action, involving first and last expenditures of some 25 billion dollars, blanketed the five cent programs of the reformers. As a result, Mr. Roosevelt was as unpopular with theologians on the left as he was with theologians on the right. The New Deal got the economy moving forward again, but it did not solve the structural problem. As late as 1935 there were 51 million Americans drawing subsistence from government pay rolls—including local governments—and government relief.[13] Up to that year, the depression had cost 50 million man-years of work lost through unemployment. As late as 1937 a special census of the unemployed in November showed 10,870,000 without work, or on government relief work. The New Deal stabilized unemployment at around 10 million, and the national income at 60 to 70 billion dollars, at a time when full employment would have produced a national income of 100 billions.

Improvisations in Control

The New Deal agencies used regulation as in the SEC; control without ownership, as in the AAA; government corporations, as in the TVA. Outright government ownership was avoided. The agencies operated where breakdowns in the economy were most severe, in banking and finance, home mortgages, agriculture, unemployment relief. They went heavily into conservation, especially after the dust storms, droughts and floods of 1935 to 1938. Dust storms boiled out of the dust bowl, which was the portion of the Great Plains ploughed up during the war for $2 wheat. The agencies went into hydroelectric power, social security legislation, wages and hours standards, and standards for collective bargaining. In due course they went into direct feeding of hungry people

13. See computation in the author's *Government in Business*, page 49.

through the Federal Surplus Commodities Corporation. Mr. Milo Perkins produced the food stamp plan, which achieved the remarkable record of a major reform having no pressure group opposing it!

The New Deal had no considered philosophy behind it. Proof is found in the violent recriminations of all those groups which espoused considered philosophies, whether deriving from Adam Smith or Karl Marx. It was a volunteer fire brigade with brooms, shovels, bath towels, dead cats, secondhand mops or anything handy with which to beat out the fire. The fire was got under control but not put out. The only revolutionary concept in the New Deal was the repudiation of the idea that the misery of the unemployed is due to their own improvidence. Fifteen million improvidents in 1933, where there had been only two million in 1929, did not make sense. The forgotten man was put in the center of the stage, and the President never wearied of advocating the cause of that third of the nation which was underfed, underhoused and inadequately clothed. Poor people kept him in office.

New Dealers had a theory about priming the pump with government investment so that private investment could take hold. It did not work out. Private investment increased, but not within billions of the amount needed to restore the old flywheel of savings-investment. Where were the opportunities for private investment on the old scale? Population growth fell to 7 per cent during the decade of the thirties, an all-time low. No great new industry like the automobile appeared on the horizon. Foreign loans were about as appealing as throwing money down the crater of Vesuvius. Where did you plan to invest 15 billions of dollars a year, gentlemen? The gentlemen had no answer except to complain that their confidence was in bad shape. Why wouldn't it be? Even little two-by-four capitalists like your author did not know where to put their money when they had any. Nobody did. So the money piled up in idle bank balances. The New Deal borrowed some of it, but not nearly enough to stimulate a job for everybody.

The New Deal has been compared to insulin given to sufferers from diabetes. The drug does not cure the disease, yet without it the patient dies.

Collapse across the Sea

The depression hit America more severely than any other country because it had farther to fall. All the world went down after 1929, with the possible exception of Russia, which had isolated its economy from world currents. The Smoot-Hawley tariff in the United States raised schedules to unprecedented heights, and threw another monkey wrench into the world free market. In 1931, Britain went off the gold standard, dragging the sterling bloc of nations along with her. Presently she abandoned her historic policy of free trade, an act which Gustav Stolper describes as an "economic earthquake." At Ottawa, members of the British Commonwealth entered into a series of agreements giving imperial preference to trade within the Empire. At the same time, Britain converted her war loan from a 5 per cent basis to 3½ per cent.

In 1931 the Kredit Anstalt failed in Vienna, and the banking system of Europe began to cave in. The Allies defaulted on their war debts to the United States. Mr. Hoover declared a moratorium on German reparations. The Young Plan, which had succeeded the Dawes Plan, which had succeeded the 33 billion dollar indemnity of Versailles, had collapsed. The skies of Brazil were grey with burning coffee. Nations which produced raw materials for the world market were in a terrible plight. Even native gatherers of chicle and wild rubber in pathless jungles were undone.

In 1936, France went off gold, dragging other nations with her. Gold ceased to function as a monetary standard, and gradually the United States buried most of the free gold in the world in the hills of Kentucky, taking it in exchange for American wheat, steel and motor cars. Nobody knew what to do with it. It was a golden elephant. Barter deals, blocked marks, blocked pounds appeared on world markets, changing multilateral trading into bilateral swaps between one country and another. Thus Britain bartered rubber for American cotton. Autarchy and economic nationalism, incipient in the 1920's, now became standard practice. Mr. Hull's trade treaties were impotent in stemming the landslide toward attempted national self-sufficiency.

The League of Nations in 1932 reported 30 million unemployed in Europe and North America. When there were 15 million jobless in the United States there were 6 million in Germany. Roosevelt stood in the rain to save America, and Hitler burned the Reichstag to offer salvation to Germans. The late Lord Lothian, Ambassador to the United States, said:[14] "The triumph of Hitler no doubt grew out of the despair which settled on central Europe in the long years of the war, defeat, inflation and revolutionary propaganda, which grew out of unemployment and frustration which followed the absence of any real unity in Europe; the sudden restriction of immigration overseas and the attempt to combine the collection of reparations and war debts by the Allies with the imposition of unjust tariffs after the war. That was what gave

14. From his last speech.

Hitler his chance." Hitler and the other dictators did not emerge bloodily from nowhere. They were the product of the same conditions which produced the New Deal. The cure may have been worse than the disease, but that is another story.

From Utopia into War

Meanwhile the ideal of the League of Nations and the brotherhood of man disintegrated rapidly as the depression gained. Nations went back to older concepts of military power. As Professor Carr points out, the nemesis of postwar utopianism came suddenly. In September 1930, Dr. Nicholas Murray Butler ventured the opinion that the world free market was again firmly established. On September 10, 1931, Lord Cecil told the League "there has scarcely ever been a period in the world's history when war seems less likely than it does at present."[15] It was all very reminiscent of the oracular statements from the highest authorities about the permanence of prosperity in 1929.

Eight days after Lord Cecil's hymn to peace, Japan invaded Manchuria. In 1935, Italy invaded Ethiopia. The economic sanctions of the League were proved worthless. In 1936, Italy, Germany and Russia intervened in Spain, and in 1937 Japan invaded China. In 1938 Hitler seized Austria, and told France and Britain at Munich what he proposed to do about Czechoslovakia—take the proposal or fight. They took it. In a few more months, the League of Nations packed up its files at Geneva and fled, leaving only a skeleton staff to rattle around in the great white palace.

The European nations went on a war basis, scrapping all

15. E. H. Carr, *op. cit.*

disarmament programs. By 1938, the world outlay in implements of war was placed at 20 billion dollars. Unemployment came to an end. The engines of prosperity began to turn again, but with what a sinister flywheel! All the experiments, the hopes, the prayers of the war to end war were laid away. Every considerable nation on earth, whether at war or at peace, reverted to the state controlled economy of 1917, where the government gave the orders and citizens obeyed.

Gold did not matter any longer, nor did debts, inflation, a favorable balance of trade. Only two questions really mattered. Have we got the fighting men; have we got the materials, especially the aircraft, to equip them? In this reversion to the starkest kind of military and economic realism, parliamentary democracy was forced to retreat. The fighting nations could not afford its cumbersome processes, the nonbelligerents looked for a strong man to lead them in their hour of peril.

A more fearsome gong than any on the stock exchange began to strike, and the panzer divisions, behind the screen of their dive bombers, rode into Poland.

THE IMPACT OF WORLD WAR II, 1939-1942

The panzer divisions released not only another world war, but a new economic tempo. Observe the astonishing effects on the United States. Back in the dear, dim days of the Presidential campaign of 1940, citizens by the millions said "you can't spend your way out of a depression." They believed it. They voted on that belief. They were supported by the highest banking, business and economic authorities. In due course, Congress appropriated 60 billion dollars, more or less, for defense spending, and Mr. Knudsen began awarding contracts as fast as God and the army bureaucrats would let him. The money flowed around the economic machine in ever greater volume. Retail sales began to jump, factories began howling for men, unemployment figures tumbled downhill, relief rolls declined, profits picked up, shortages developed in machine tools and certain types of skilled labor, prices began to climb for many products—the backbone of the depression was broken. The President, Congress and Mr. Knudsen had combined "to spend our way out of it." Oh, but the terrible government debt? Another 7 billion dollars goes for the Lend-Lease bill! Oh, but the budget, the budget? Another 9 billions goes for the army!

There is no business depression in Britain, Canada, Australia, Germany, Italy, Japan, in any nation where armament expenditures are large. Consumers are rationed for many commodities, but money is racing around the economic circuit. Governments are now claiming and spending anywhere from 20 to 70 per cent of national income. In all belligerent countries the figure soon climbs to well above 50 per cent. In England there are only 200 persons left who receive as much as $20,000 a year, after taxes. In the great bull market, thousands of Americans used to clean up $20,000 in a five-hour trading day.

Congress before the attack on Pearl Harbor had already appropriated more than twice as much money for guns as the New Deal spent for butter, and other things, in eight years to 1940. It had appropriated more than twice as much as was spent for guns in the last war, when we shipped two million men to France. Where's the money coming from? Nobody gives a damn. That is just the point. In the old economy, such reckless outlays would have spelled bankruptcy and ruin. Money came first and men came second. In the new economy, no nation will permit bankruptcy and ruin so long as men, materials and energy are available. Men first, money second.

You do not understand how this can be so? I will try to explain. Germany does not permit ruin and bankruptcy and has little use for gold. It is Germany we are up against now. Adam Smith may heave in his grave, but no nation in this dangerous world of 1942 is meekly going bankrupt because some textbooks say it ought to. It will go physically bankrupt when it runs out of food, coal, iron, oil, aluminum, and not before. Well, who is going to pay for it? It is being paid for right now with the mental and physical work of those who are producing and moving the goods. "Stuff and nonsense," you cry, your eye on the book. Put your book away, my friend. The books which will explain the new world we are entering have not been written.

Germany

In 1933, Germany had at least 6 million unemployed, practically no monetary gold, meagre foreign exchange with which to buy goods abroad, and unlimited debts. The state was bankrupt under the old rules. Hitler seized power, and he appointed Dr. Hjalmar Schacht to figure out a set of new rules. Here were all those idle men; why shouldn't they produce something useful? Dr. Schacht borrowed an idea or two from John Maynard Keynes, the British economist, and went to work. He devised a new pegged fiat money system, based on industrial and agricultural production. The more production, the more money. Here was the way to absorb the unemployed. He revived foreign trade by the invention of blocked marks. He bought grain from the Balkans, for instance, and gave money for it which was only good in Germany for the purchase of industrial goods. Balkan peasants were flat on their backs in the world depression, and were glad to move their products with any kind of money. Later on they found that they might get only mouth organs and glass eye balls for their wheat.

A Four Year Plan was adopted (Russia had a Five Year Plan) with the aim of maximum self-sufficiency for the German economy, essential raw materials to be obtained by the blocked mark device. The state took control of prices, wages, profits. Inflation was *verboten,* and has not developed to this day. Labor unions and employers' associations were abolished. In due time, all labor was conscripted. Wages were pegged at 1932 levels. Agriculture was rigorously controlled. From 1933 to 1938, armament production was increased 300 per cent, consumer goods 33 per cent. Two million new homes for workers were built, great highways constructed. Two years after Dr. Schacht began operations, the 6 million idle were all at work. Soon a labor shortage developed which is still acute, in spite of work levies drawn from prisoners of war. Capitalists and businessmen were not eliminated *but they lost the power of making important decisions.* Profits are earned by private companies, often ample ones. But those who receive the profits are not permitted to withhold them from active use. They must put the profits back into circulation either by expanding plant or by purchasing government bonds. The essential point is that profits are no longer the spark plug of the economic system. In capitalism, profits are what make the system tick. In Germany they are just another part of the national income. The idea that the Nazi economy was a decadent form of capitalism came chiefly from Marxist debaters. Power has passed completely out of the hands of capitalists in Germany.

Japan

Japan has copied many elements of the German system. She can permit no Fuehrer, for he would compete with the symbol of the Emperor, which is unthinkable. She has a one-party government and a planned economy. This system is aimed with deadly efficiency at the increase of armaments, and the restriction of consumer goods to release purchasing power for buying government bonds. Prices, rents, wages, return on investments, are fixed by the state. There has been some inflation but no serious situation has developed. Luxury goods are banned. The government has taken over the entire shipping industry and fixes its prices and wages. Big business is not in the doghouse, as in Germany, but it is not on the front porch, either. Standards of living of the rich are declining rapidly, as in Britain.

The United States

The United States has just declared war as I write. Business as usual is rapidly becoming unrecognizable. Vast stores of material are being lent or leased to Britain, Russia, China. Farm exports have all but ceased except under lend-lease subsidy. The government has commandeered merchant shipping, and now controls 95 per cent of exports through licenses. From another direction, the government moves on the most cherished of all American products, the motor car, by ordering the complete elimination of passenger car production.

Congress has passed a law permitting the seizure of property in specified categories necessary for the national defense. Conscription has been extended to two years and a half. The RFC is building or helping to build six billion dollars' worth of new industrial plants, while the government is preparing to double aluminum capacity by advancing the money for seven large new plants. The steel industry is being expanded under government pressure, and plans are ready for an enormous development of synthetic rubber production as war in the Far East cuts off the natural supply. Women have rioted for silk stockings in the stores as the Japanese silk trade has been stopped dead. Nylon, rayon, cotton, must move into the place abandoned by raw silk, turning the textile industry upside down.

Serious shortages have developed in magnesium, zinc, copper, brass, tin, tungsten, nickel, chromium, manganese, lead, wool, cork, kapok, toluene and certain strategic chemicals.[16] The government has been forced to ration these materials with an elaborate system of priorities, in which defense needs come first and, if there is any left, consumer needs come second. Consumers will have increasing difficulty in buying not only automobiles, but refrigerators, washing machines, furnaces, hardware, ranges, kitchen utensils—anything which contains even traces of the metals now growing scarce. The Federal Reserve Board has made it easier for consumers to practice self-restraint by tightening up intallment buying, with higher down payments and shorter terms for payment.

Mr. Leon Henderson is putting price ceilings on products right and left, so that shortages will not take their "normal" course in runaway prices. In some cases, such as silk, the gov-

16. See article in *Fortune* for August 1941, summarizing the situation for each material.

ernment has taken physical control of all visible stocks. A comprehensive and drastic price control and anti-inflation bill is just around the corner. The idea is that if Germany can fight a war without inflation, why can't we. Meanwhile, the country is developing a bad case of "priorities unemployment," due to shortages in raw materials for consumer goods, and drastic steps are contemplated to remedy that. The awarding of defense contracts primarily to large companies has jeopardized the position of thousands of small concerns. The cutting down of durable goods for consumers has jeopardized the position of tens of thousands of retail dealers, especially automobile and tire dealers. The American economy can hardly avoid squeezing out of business a large number of small concerns in the next few years, thus taking another long step in the direction of centralization.

The army, with bayonets fixed, has marched into an aircraft plant on the west coast, dispersed a picket line, and taken over. The navy has taken over a strike-bound shipbuilding plant on the east coast. The marines were not needed. Before the crisis is over, many observers think that strikes in defense industries will be banned by law. What is that going to do to the principle of collective bargaining?

Even before the President's last message about 10 per cent of our man power was in the army or making munitions. By the summer of 1942 it is estimated that the rate will have jumped to 27 per cent, with 15 million persons engaged in war work. In 1943, Mr. Roosevelt prophesies, we shall spend half of our national income for war. In October 1940, there were 204,000 workers in the aircraft industry, and for early 1942 the estimate is 859,000.[17] In September 1941, the back-

17. U. S. Bureau of Labor Statistics estimates in June 1941.

log, or unfilled orders, of the airplane industry topped 7 billion dollars. The Federal Power Commission estimates that power capacity will be stepped up from the present 42 million kilowatts to 64 million kilowatts by 1946—an increase of 50 per cent in the national energy supply. Private power plant capacity will increase by 40 per cent; public power by 100 per cent. The TVA is building half a dozen great new dams. These estimates have the utility people worried on two counts: How deep is government getting in the power picture? What are we going to do with all this energy after the war?

The new bomber program will carve out as big a section in the American economy as the whole automobile industry occupied! This is only a starter. The new tank program will be as big as General Motors! The new shipbuilding program calls for shipyard capacity greater than that of the whole world in peace times!

As the American economy becomes increasingly distorted from its accustomed pattern under this shattering impact, a curious phenomenon emerges. All the wealth of Croesus will not buy a pound of aluminum when there is no aluminum available. Hitherto, one could always get what he wanted if he was prepared to pay the price. From now on, price will become a *secondary* matter as commodity after commodity goes under priority and rationing control. The fundamental physical basis of all economic systems moves into clear perspective for government official, businessman, banker, wage earner and housewife to see. The WPB and the Board of Economic Warfare are thinking almost exclusively in term of materials—pounds, tons, barrels, bales, square feet—who is going to get them, and how long they are going to last. For many years such perspective has been blurred by a capacity to produce far in excess of normal demand, with the result that people came to think that purchasing power, in terms of money, was the prime consideration. Now we are in a period where the amount of steel, copper, aluminum, raw silk, lead, zinc, kilo-watts of energy, appear as the prime considerations—which of course they are, and always have been. In brief, we are in for a strong dose of physical economics, which promises to be very educational and not a little painful.

The Conscription of Capital

Mr. A. Feiler, in a recent study of war economy,[18] notes that a point comes in the war or defense effort where produc-tion can no longer be increased. Then the state must begin to restrict civilian consumption. This point has already been reached in the United States for certain goods, with more to come. (In some cases it has been reached *before* possible steps to increase production have been taken, as in the case of steel.) As a last resort, the state can "mine" the economy, by tearing into soils, forests and mineral deposits, slaughtering cattle, letting the industrial plant run down. "A long total war is a vast process of erosion." Germany, Britain, Russia, Italy and Japan have entered this stage already, where wealth is being destroyed faster than it is being created.

In a war emergency, the state can conscript or control cap-ital in at least nine ways. It can:

1. Prevent the flight of capital and currency abroad.
2. Register foreign securities held by individuals, take them over, giving local bonds or money instead.
3. Set up a foreign trade monopoly, embargoing exports.
4. Establish priorities for the delivery of raw materials.

18. *Social Research*, February 1941.

5. Fix prices or price ceilings in bottleneck industries.
6. Ration materials directly.
7. Control labor and ultimately conscript it.
8. Set up a system of forced loans.
9. Inaugurate compulsory cartels and mergers.

Germany and Britain are far along these nine roads; the
United States is entering them. In this control-without-owner-
ship agenda, "the whole concept of capital and property becomes meaningless."

Mr. Feiler concludes: "The conscription of property will
not end with the war, but will actually be of immensely greater importance in the ensuing peace," as the mass of the people
and the army demand adequate living standards and full employment. "This war is a social and economic world revolution. This may still sound radical to some; they will find the
truth of it later, by experience."

Britain, Canada, Australia have gone farther along the path
of planned economy than has the United States, though not
yet so far as Japan, Germany, Italy and Russia. France is on a
similar road, and so are Turkey, Sweden, Switzerland and
Finland. So are Mexico, Brazil, Argentina. China is far gone
in centralized state control.

Is there a nation left on earth where enterprise is free? The
United States is the most free and I have cited a brief record
of what has come here, and is coming. Politically, socially,
the differences between nations are wide. Economically the
pattern becomes standard. Total war, total defense, even a
total battle against depression, demand it. The pattern has
been taking shape for a quarter of a century. For better or for
worse, it is the curve which we must now ride out.

Whether a planned economy can make people happier than

a system of free enterprise is open for debate. That planned economies are coming so fast you can hear the wind whistle around their edges, is not a debatable proposition.

2

INVENTORY OF BASIC TRENDS
1914—1942

I HAVE GIVEN a fast movie of a quarter of a century of economic history. One major theme runs through it: the massive shift from an economy where businessmen made most of the important decisions to an economy where government men make most of the important decisions. Sometimes, as in the case of Mr. Donald Nelson, the same man makes the new decisions. The shift may be slow or rapid, but it goes on relentlessly in every nation on earth.

In the first World War it started slowly and then accelerated, until something close to totalitarian economies were operating by 1918. In the uneasy peace which followed the war, only the United States turned most of its major economic decisions back to businessmen. Other countries expanded their programs of social legislation, and sought by government controls to promote economic self-sufficiency. Even in the United States, government activities were considerably increased over the 1913 level by highway and school construction, traffic control and the expansion of many social services, especially in cities. Great corporations in the United States broke away from the free market, and began to "administer" prices, contrary to all the doctrines of laissez faire.

In the world depression, governments everywhere were forced to intervene to keep banks from closing, farmers from revolting, people from starving. The current World War begins where the last one left off, with totalitarian state controls in all belligerent countries, and in many neutrals. The United States moves steadily in the same direction.

Suppose we reach a hand, as it were, into the history just recorded, and pick out certain trends for special examination. Perhaps they will help to throw some light on the great transition which began with the last war and is now going with throttle wide open. The trends we will discuss fall roughly into two groups:

1. Prime causes for social change.
2. Effects produced by these causes.

Causes: Technological Advance

The industrial revolution destroyed the set of institutions known as feudalism, and inaugurated the institutions called capitalism. Applied science has thus already engineered one vast transition. There is good reason to believe that the same cause is a major factor in engineering the present transition. It is certainly the cause for precipitating what has been called the economy of abundance, with the resulting paradox of poverty in the midst of plenty. A very loose generalization might be that a moderate injection of inanimate energy into an economic system produces capitalism, and a great deal of it produces collectivism.

There is no question about the acceleration of inanimate energy. Energy consumed per capita in the United States increased 40-fold from 1830 to 1930. In 1910, we produced about 300 million barrels of petroleum, in 1940 about 1,300 million. With the building of huge government and utility company dams, water power has enormously increased in the last quarter century. A great part of the 40-fold increase in energy consumption has come since World War I.

There is no question about the acceleration of invention. In the decade ending in 1890, 208,000 patents were granted in the United States. In the decade ending in 1910, 314,000. In the decade ending in 1930, 421,000.

The two most important indices of technology are energy consumption and the rate of invention. Energy permits machines to perform tasks once performed by men. As it increases, it drives down the costs of production. The *reductio ad absurdum* of the process is a handful of switch-throwers turning out all the goods the nation needs. The threat to vested rights in jobs, and to vested financial rights in obsolete processes, is obviously severe. We do not need to look any farther for a major cause of unemployment, of agricultural surpluses, of excess plant capacity and a falling rate of interest. Down comes the cost, and up goes the output per man-hour. The rate of invention meanwhile determines the rate of change in social habits and behavior. Consider what the invention of the automobile alone has done to day-by-day habits in America. Consider what the invention of the airplane has done to warfare. If the rate of invention continues high, rapid changes in behavior, bringing economic, political and ideological changes in their train, are inevitable. In a very real sense the world has not gone crazy since 1914; it has just stepped up the rate of social change to correspond with the rate of invention.

Here is an inventory of energy sources in recent years. Look at the pitiful place occupied by human muscle.

[19]From coal	17,000	trillion BTU a year
From oil	6,500	"
From water power	1,900	"
From natural gas	1,700	"
From firewood	1,600	"
From draft animals	750	"
From *man power*	400	"
From windmills	300	"

The machine age of coal, iron and smoke-bound cities is being gradually replaced by the power age of electric power, light metals and decentralized factories. In the machine age, the craftsman gives way to the human robot with his soul-killing repetitive motions. In the power age, the robot gives way to the highly educated inspector, and to the photoelectric cell. The current war will speed up power age techniques. Potential output at its conclusion promises to be stupendous.

Technology is advancing not only in mechanical fields, but in agrobiology, crop genetics, the chemistry of fertilizers and scientific methods generally for making ten blades of grass grow where one grew before. This reduces the number of farmers needed to feed the community. Technology is advancing in scientific management and in psychological problems of employment. A fifteen-year study by the Western Electric Company of the motives which lie behind human work, promises to revolutionize employer-employee relations some day, and greatly increase output per man-hour—all without the aid of a single new machine.

Causes: The Flattening Population Curve

We use words to separate things so that our minds can handle them, but reality is indivisible. Technology reacts on

19. Computation by the author in *The Economy of Abundance*, 1934.

the birth rate, the death rate and migration, the three deter-
minants of population growth, and population growth in turn
reacts on technology. For instance, rapid city growth speeds
invention in skyscrapers, elevators, subways, traffic controls.
The abnormal increase in population in the nineteenth century was due in large part to the industrial revolution, and
was thus a direct effect of technology. A declining death rate,
due to medical science, also had its effect.

The lagging population curve is due primarily to the fact
that children are economic liabilities in high-energy societies.
In handicraft days they began to help around the farm as
soon as they could walk. Let the reader ask himself what economic contribution to the family livelihood his children have
made, at least until they have finished school. And when they
leave school, can they get a job? People still want children,
right enough, but the net cost is higher than many a willing
parent can afford.

Technical methods of controlling births are now widely
known, and the birth rate in Western civilization has been
falling for many decades. Later marriages, city living, have
helped to push it down. In Western Europe, population will
probably reach a peak in the next few years and then decline
—unless the war reduces the peak. In the United States, the
peak will probably be reached not later than 1960. For decade
after decade our population increased 30 per cent and more.
About the time of the Civil War this rate began to slacken
off. By the 1920's it was down to 16 per cent. The Census of
1940 establishes an all-time low of a 7 per cent growth for
the decade ended in that year. Part of this change is due to the
virtual cessation of immigration. When we remember that
real estate values are a function of population growth, we

catch a hint of the profound effects that a slackening of that growth has made, and is going to make, on the economic system.

Census estimates, following Thompson and Whelpton, show that while we now have 45,000,000 young people under twenty, in 1980 we shall have only some 34,000,000. The decline in the under-twenty group is already being felt in schools all over the country. Between 1930 and 1940, elementary schools in New York City lost 150,000 pupils. Teaching staffs were cut down; school budgets shrank. On the other side of the ledger, where we have 9,000,000 citizens over 65 today, by 1980 we shall have 22,000,000. In the light of these figures, the rise of the Townsend Old-Age Plan becomes clearer. The political and economic effects of these shifting age groups promise to be great.

Causes: The Closing Frontier

During the eighteenth and nineteenth centuries, four continents and countless islands of the sea were opened up for colonization, trade and investment. By 1900, no more free lands were available for homesteading in the United States, while the Great Powers had staked out claims in all real estate not already occupied by another Great Power. It has been well said that capitalism could have continued happily through the twentieth century if ways and means had been available to colonize the moon.

During the nineteenth century, the growing population swarmed into the growing colonial areas, into the great American West, into Australia, South America, and provided steadily expanding markets for investments at home and abroad. You could not lose if you played the game shrewdly;

you bought in at the ten million population mark and sold out at the twenty million mark. American history could be written in terms of a gigantic real estate boom. The curve sagged a bit when speculators overextended themselves, but it always went up again.

In the year 1920, American farm land values reached their peak. Canny owners sold out and went to Southern California. These values, in most areas, have been coming down ever since. Free land stimulates population, and both stimulate business expansion and opportunities for profitable investment. For a hundred years in this country, the expansion when plotted approximated a 3 to 4 per cent compound interest curve. On this curve, the free enterprise system flourished like a green bay tree. When the curve heads downward, investors are nonplussed, and presently lose their confidence.

Effects: Interdependence

In early New England villages, our forefathers produced upwards of 90 per cent of all their needs with their own hands, and the hands of their neighbors. In Boston today, most families do not produce one per cent of the things they consume. Work has been specialized in factories, in mines, on farms; an enormous army has entered the service trades just to push the specialized output around; with the result that every person in the American community—or any high-energy society—is dependent upon literally millions of other people for his daily necessities.

We are all bound into two vast exchange networks: the network of goods and services, the network of money and credit. Both must be functioning efficiently if the community is to eat. Both were almost unknown in low-energy societies.

People without money could still eat, for they found their food within range of their eyes.

When the networks are operating well, standards of living for the average citizen are higher than kings could enjoy in earlier ages. Charlemagne had no electric lights, automobiles, moving picture palaces or oil burning furnaces. When the networks are operating badly, the average citizen's standard of living goes out from under him, while his mental anguish is greater than any his forefathers knew. In 1929, the financial network collapsed, though the physical network was in good order. I have earlier recorded the effects on the people of Sunnyside—multiply them for nearly every local community in the country. In a recent blizzard in my part of the country, the physical network collapsed in the form of electric power. For a week we froze and groped in the dark; some families nearly starved. Farmers who still relied on wood stoves, well buckets, root cellars and kerosene lamps, were snug and comfortable.

Somebody must be responsible for keeping both networks operating regularly, or the very survival of modern communities is threatened. Here is one principal reason for economic interference by the state. If the free enterprise system cannot do the job automatically, then the state must do it deliberately. That is precisely what President Roosevelt did when he got the banking network functioning again in 1933.

Effects: Unemployment

The advance of technology often costs men and women their jobs. The phenomenon is called technological unemployment. Books have been filled with the evidence, and we do not need to recapitulate here. One dramatic case was that of theatre musicians displaced by the talkies in the late 1920's. But technology also makes jobs—look at the new airplane industry. Which pull is the stronger? The consensus of opinion seems to be that they about cancelled each other out until the 1920's, but since then technological unemployment has been getting ahead. It seems a reasonable conclusion, with labor-saving inventions going like a house afire, and with not many large new industries arising to absorb the shock. (The war program will change the trend, while it lasts.)

We must not forget, furthermore, that even if new jobs are made as fast as old jobs are lost, the new job may be in Seattle, the old one in Pittsburgh, and Tom Adams in Pittsburgh has not got the carfare. . . . Or maybe he has not got the skill. . . . Or maybe he cannot sell his house and move the family. A high rate of technological unemployment produces shattering misery in the interval between jobs. A net balance may please statisticians, but hardly the victims of the process.

A far greater volume of unemployment arises from business depressions. Depressions come chiefly from failure of opportunities for investment, thus closing down the heavy industries, and presently careening the whole economy. Failure of investment opportunities is tied up with population trends, the frontier, and technology again.

Whatever the prime cause, unemployment is the chief cancer in modern society. It frustrates and enrages people beyond anything else. If Germany had not had a terrible unemployment problem in 1933, Hitler would never have come to power. Here, unemployment was a direct cause of the New Deal.

Effects: The Decline of Investment Opportunities
Take the city you are living in, or the one nearest you.

Apart from special war activities, is the population growing? Are new skyscrapers being erected? Are factories moving in and enlarging their capacity? Are real estate values going up? Unless you live in certain parts of California or Florida, your answer to these questions will be "No." Your city is not fulfilling the cheery prognostications of its Chamber of Commerce a decade ago.

Now let me ask you another group of questions: Is your city perfect as it stands? Has it slums which should be torn down, water fronts which should be cleaned up and made into parks, streets which should be widened so that one can find a place to park, hospitals which should be improved, playgrounds which should be built, traffic problems which should be unsnarled, river pollution which should be eliminated, a smoke nuisance which should be abated? To most of these questions, and others like them, you will answer "Yes."

This is the problem of investment in a nutshell. Alvin Hansen calls the first construction of your city *extensive* investment; the clearing of the wilderness, laying out of streets, bringing in the railroads, construction of houses, stores, office buildings, warehouses, factories, docks, utilities. Here was a rich field for private investment, with fine risks to be taken for profit or loss, with odds on the profits. Now your city has almost ceased to grow. Its pioneering days are over. But is it finished? A thousand times no. It is rough, crude, ugly in many areas, with wretched living conditions in others. The time has come to make it a better city, not a bigger one. Such investment Dr. Hansen calls *intensive*. It does not appeal much to takers of risks; it does not attract private capital. If slums are to be torn down, parks, playgrounds, schools, hospitals improved, the government must do most of it. Intensive investments are more in the nature of social capital. The interest rate is very low, the element of speculation almost absent.

After the war the United States could use many billions of intensive investment annually for generations, keeping everyone employed in adapting cities to the power age, checking soil erosion, replanting forests and grass cover, extending medical care and education, rehousing that part of the population which now lives in reeking tenements and tarpaper shacks. What a country we could make, and how our young people would delight in making it! See how eagerly CCC boys accept the responsibility. But if these things are to be done, the government must arrange for most of their financing. You dare not attempt it with your money, nor I with mine.

Where are we going to put our savings when the war is over? The disposition of savings has been worrying us for twelve years. It has been worrying Europeans for a generation. Our worries have been eloquently reflected in a falling rate of interest. Intensive investments can thrive on a one per cent basis; the lower the better. Extensive investments thrive on high interest rates.

Let us recapitulate the causes for the decline in opportunities for private investment:

1. The lagging population curve.
2. The closing of the frontier in the United States.
3. The high mortality rate in loans abroad.
4. The condition of excess capacity in many industries, even in 1929.
5. Falling farm land values and surplus crops. Who wants to invest in orange groves, when good oranges are dumped to rot in mile-long piles?
6. Technology is constantly increasing the efficiency of a dollar of

new investment. When Isador Lubin at the TNEC hearings asked Alfred P. Sloan, Jr., of General Motors, whether a piece of equipment today, costing $1,000, would yield a greater output than a similar machine costing $1,000 fifteen years ago, Mr. Sloan replied: "Unquestionably. It is astounding the progress which has been made."

The largest absorber of capital in the 1920's was the automobile industry. It looks like intensive investment. In part it was. But in another sense it was extensive investment, for the motor car opened new geographical frontiers. It enabled people to live in places, and do business in areas, never before exploited, and it fostered a substantial expansion in suburban and country houses, filling stations, roadside industries, decentralized plants. A cheap airplane which anyone could fly might expand the frontier again. Will we get it after the war?

Effects: The Decline of the Free Market

It may or may not be significant that serious attempts to control prices and restrict production were made by great corporations, cartels and trade associations, just at the time the rate of expansion began to decline. People usually associate the monopoly movement with a selfish desire to increase profits. May it not have been impelled even more by a desire to avoid losses? Certainly the mergers and combinations were not formed by wicked men determined to destroy the free market. They were mostly formed by men who had a faith almost religious in the free market ideology—for instance, Mr. Wendell Willkie. Circumstances over which they had little or no control led them into amalgamation, large-scale operations and administered prices. Mass production was obviously one reason.

The free market, at home and abroad, was born in a period of vigorous expansion, and presently Adam Smith gave it suitable ideological garments. The garments remain, but the market languishes, both abroad and at home. That is the reason why Mr. Willkie could honestly advocate things he had long since ceased to do in his own company. Stockholders are not interested in ideological dividends.

The prime causes, listed above, undermined the automatic functioning of the free market. The first World War distorted it further. Businessmen, with their cartels, national and international, gave it a terrible mangling. Big business without formal monopoly—"oligopoly" as we termed it earlier— made wide inroads into the free market all during the 1920's. Messrs. Harding, Coolidge and Hoover were ardent admirers of laissez faire, and permitted a minimum of government interference. I think it fair to say that governments have not been chiefly responsible for the decline of the free market. Other causes, including businessmen themselves, have been more responsible. When the automatic mechanism ceased to function, governments came in as a kind of lifeguard crew to keep the community from drowning. This is very clear in the case of Mr. Hoover, forced by the depression to take steps at right angles to his philosophy.

Effects: High-Pressure Talk

In the production of material goods, continents, if not nations, have recently become more self-sufficient with the invention of synthetics, substitutes, ersatz commodities. In the production of talk, one sits before a radio and listens to war commentators in London, Cairo, Batavia and Berne, in a fifteen-minute roundup, which still finds time to emphasize the virtues of the world's fastest selling single-edge razor blade, and the world's most honored watch. The Germans may be the enemies of civilization, but when Harry W. Flannery of CBS interviews Max Schmeling (the boy who knocked out Joe Louis) in a Greek hospital after he has descended by parachute on Crete, suddenly all men are brothers for five minutes, radio time.

Technology is the prime cause for this talk, which travels around the earth at the speed of light. It is the cause of Sunday morning papers which come out on Saturday afternoon, of instant communication between all arms engaged in a battle, of fireside chats, sound-wagons, lives saved by SOS and lives lost by U-boats. Trade may decrease, but communication is speeded up. It is arguable that neither Hitler nor Roosevelt could have held power without the radio. All German military campaigns now dovetail with the assault by propaganda. Other nations tag along as best they can.

Science is responsible not only for the speed of transmission from mouth to ear drum, but for a lot of the word combinations coming out of the mouth. The whole bag of psychology has been up-ended and shaken out to provide word patterns which can make people do things they had not planned to do, buy things they have no use for, believe things they never thought possible, see things which are not there, fear things which do not exist, hope for things which are unattainable. Governments, tooth paste manufacturers, social workers, churches, glamour girls, college presidents, whiskey dealers, ballplayers, stuffed shirts—all are privy to the techniques, through the ministrations of their publicity experts. Dr. Goebbels learns from Ivy Lee, and Sir Gerald Campbell learns from Dr. Goebbels.

It is apparently the firm intention of all these distinguished gentlemen to prevent any person on the planet from ever having a thought of his own. If it were not for the fact that many of their spells cancel each other out, they would be far on the road to success. Indeed that is humanity's hope. The propaganda will become so intense, from so many directions, that it will all cancel out.[20] People will become immune, like the generations exposed to smallpox. Or else, prodded by so many contrary stimuli, they will go crazy, like Pavlov's dogs.

We are riding high on the propaganda curve today, and no man can say where that ride will end. Sometimes I think it is the most dangerous of all modern trends. It had its large-scale beginning in the first World War, and was magnificently perfected in the Circassian walnut cubicles of American advertising agencies during the era of normalcy. Dr. Goebbels picked it up from there.

Effects: Mechanized Warfare

The bombing airplane is a child of technology, and promises to revolutionize the maps of the world. It has destroyed the French Republic, rocked the mighty British Empire, consolidated Europe under one tyranny, and is fast consolidating the Western Hemisphere and all its outlying islands into a unified system of defense. It has shattered the established concepts of sea power, and made the doctrine of the freedom of the seas impossible to enforce. It has sent the *Prince of Wales* to the bottom and sooner or later it will make the battleship obsolete. It has wrecked the principle of self-determination and the rights and sovereignties of small

20. A good illustration is the way the official German and Russian war bulletins cancelled out during the first months of combat.

nations. If you have the bombers and the fighting planes, you can protect your sovereignty. Otherwise it must be surrendered to the protection of those who do have the bombers.

The bombing plane, combined with other new devices of mechanical destruction, is destined violently to shrink the number of nations with full sovereign rights. There were sixty in 1939. How many will there be by the time this war has run its course?[21]

Effects: Government in Business

Technological pressures, a slowing population curve, the closing of frontiers for investment, have helped to produce the series of profound social effects just described. These effects, especially those threatening community survival, have produced other effects. The most important is the wholesale invasion by the state of areas hitherto reserved for private business. There is as yet no name for this invasion. It is not socialism in the orthodox sense; it is not fascism defined as the last stand of big business; it is not the cooperative commonwealth. What is it? For the moment all we can do is to call it "X."

The proletarians are not running the governments, even in Russia. Businessmen as such are not running them. It has been suggested that a new class of "managers" is beginning to run them.[22] The managers are recruited from government service, business concerns, labor organizations, the professions, the universities. They are not politicians after gravy but technicians and trained administrators after power. The WPB comes to mind, and the 1,000 technicians who are said to constitute Hit-

21. See quote from Lord Lothian on page 77.
22. See James Burnham, *The Managerial Revolution.*

ler's brain trust. This is all highly speculative, as the situation is very much in flux, but it is an ingenious explanation.

Whoever is running the several governments, matters have now progressed so far that any retreat from an era of planned economy is remote. The trend promises to be with us for a long time to come. In Russia, the planning extends to all parts of the economic machine; in Germany it extends to most parts, but permits bankers and businessmen to go through motions; in Sweden it extends to all key points, especially financial controls; in the United States—up to the attack on Pearl Harbor—it extended to finance, agriculture, natural resources, energy, social security legislation and jobs for the unemployed. Somewhere between Russia on the left, and the United States on the right, the pattern of other nations falls.

Parliamentary democracy is under pressure as state intervention gains. The world of 1942 calls for swift decisions and swift action. Parliaments and legislatures are slow in getting four or five hundred men to come to a decision. Powerful pressure groups, furthermore, are given full play in parliamentary democracies and often hold up action. Their lobbyists bedevil legislators and administrators, often to the point where little work can be done. I know an exceedingly able administrator in Washington, more than half of whose time is wasted in calming down people with axes to grind.

Some pressure groups oppose every piece of major legislation, however beneficent it may be for the community as a whole, and kill it if they can. They kept the child labor law kicking around for twenty years. When defeated in Congress they appeal to the courts and seek to have the act declared unconstitutional, or at least subjected to interminable delays. Over five hundred lobbies are registered in Washington. Yet pressure group politics is traditional, legal, respectable and to a degree necessary under our democratic system.

The totalitarians have cut through all this pulling and hauling. Legislatures have been dispersed, except to meet once a year and say "Yes, sir!" The men at the top are in a position to make quick decisions and take quick action. In getting this freedom of action, however, they have been forced to sacrifice many things which make a community loyal and contented. Their actions have to be good or the situation will ultimately get out of hand. Maybe a "slave" economy can be run in wartime, but not over the long years of peace; not in the power age.

I have no theories as to how this trend is going to work out. I hope with all my heart that democratic procedures can be modified so that swifter action can be taken, without crippling the fundamental democratic structure. In wartime, of course, there is no problem. Modern democracies, as we have seen, must go totalitarian, too, so far as centralized decisions are concerned. Mr. Wilson learned the lesson in 1917.

Effects: Autarchy or National Self-Sufficiency

On November 27, 1938, the late Lord Lothian wrote in the London *Observer:*

Though few realize it, the old anarchy of multitudinous national sovereignties is about to dissolve and quickly . . . The great military powers, either by compulsion or by the magnetic attraction of their own strength, will consolidate a group of otherwise autonomous units, to whom they promise peace, security and prosperity in return for entering their orbit. . . . That the world is going to fall into four or five political and economic groups, each in a great measure self-supporting, each under the leadership of a great state equipped with modern military airpower, seems certain . . . Nothing we can do can prevent it.

Note the noble lord's emphasis on the bombing plane. It is a pity he did not help Britain get more of them in 1938.

Autarchy is a condition where the national government steps into the field of foreign trade to specify what commodities shall be exported and imported, in line with a strong policy of national self-sufficiency. It is in direct conflict with all the principles of the world free market, where trade is carried on by individual businessmen, buying in the cheapest market and selling in the dearest.

The United States government has practiced a kind of autarchy for generations by means of its high tariffs. It has shut out imports, or made them prohibitively costly. An Italian economist, Luigi Villari, takes the position, and I think it is justified, that this has stimulated autarchy elsewhere. "Naturally," he says, "the United States is perfectly free to establish all the customs and other restrictions it chooses. . . . But Americans should not be surprised by the inevitable retaliations of countries who are hard hit by those measures. Nor should they call those reactions immoral and conflicting with the canons of international society. Italian and German autarchy is the direct consequence of measures taken by the United States and a few other countries. The result was that many products which formerly came from abroad are now being manufactured at home."

Autarchy has been promoted also by the development of international cartels which have controlled world supplies of tin, rubber, sugar, copper, or what have you. This naturally frightens governments. What if the cartel cuts off our supply? So the government goes to work to make itself independent of the cartel, or even better, gets control of the cartel. Autarchy has been promoted by the invention of synthetics and by the pressure of competition.

Scientists are now constructing synthetic materials from atomic bricks. The Germans can turn coal into butter. Dupont takes coal, water and air and produces silk stockings. If the United States loses its raw rubber supply from the Far East, it can in two years' time begin to make all the rubber it wants out of petroleum, at a not much greater cost. Clearly if this kind of invention continues, it will not be long before any nation with enough energy available, can become self-sufficient in many raw materials, without bothering about foreign trade. Germany, Italy, Japan may be marching out to seize things which they presently will not need. By the same token, the British may be defending an Empire whose usefulness as a reservoir of raw materials is passing. Historians may some day record that, economically, this was the most needless war ever fought.

"The free traders preach, the autarchists practice." Mr. Hull laid down beautiful principles which nobody was willing to observe. The autarchist has no principles at all except to obtain enough goods to keep his community afloat, and especially to safeguard his supplies in time of war. So he goes in for maximum self-sufficiency and a minimum dependence on trade routes which can be bombed or torpedoed.

From the point of view of the whole community, this may or may not be more costly. In a depression, it is desirable to keep the home labor force employed, even if the cost of production is higher than for imported goods. Otherwise the laborers go on relief and the community pays anyway. Is it better to have the shoemakers of Brockton walking the streets, or to bar out Czechoslovak shoes and give them work?

Whatever the morals and whatever the comparative costs, autarchy has been gaining steadily since the last war. It should be noted, however, that this trend is now working in the direction of larger home units. Germany is taking down customs barriers in Europe; Japan is taking them down in the Far East; the United States is merging its economy with that of Canada, and presently—who knows?—with much of Latin America.

While the trend is unmistakably in the direction of continental blocs, largely self-sufficient, a qualification is distinctly in order. If the twenty-six United Nations under their pact of January 1942 destroy the military power of the Axis, an attempt will probably be made to set up a new world order dominated by the United States, Britain and Russia. It will have to be a much firmer structure than the League of Nations, if it is to succeed, with all participants surrendering sovereignty to a central police power.

Conclusions

Let us recapitulate the eleven great economic trends of our age, with a note on the time factors involved:

1. The advance of *technology*. This curve has been operating for more than a century. There is no end in sight. If Uranium 235 becomes a practical source of atomic power, the economic effects will surpass anything yet produced by science.

2. The halting curve of *population*. It began to halt toward the close of the nineteenth century, and the decline in growth rate will probably continue until stable populations, or even declining ones, are reached in Europe and America, within the next generation.

3. The closing *frontier* in the United States. After 1890, the government dispersed almost no more free land.

4. Growing *interdependence*. This curve began to move even before Watt's steam engine was invented, and will continue to move briskly for some time to come. Synthetics and substitutes are checking it a little, and may check it more in the future. But the independent family unit, in the early New England sense, has gone, probably forever.

5. The gathering threat of *unemployment*. This is the major reason for social unrest and the revolutionary urge toward security. Chronic unemployment was not in evidence in Europe before World War I. It reached the United States in 1930.

6. The decline in private *investment opportunities*. It appeared in parts of Europe after the war, in the United States after 1929. There is no sign that the curve will reverse its course for years to come.

7. The decline of the *free market*. It began with the trusts of the 1880's, and became acute with the administered price era of the 1920's. There is no sign that this curve will reverse itself either.

8. The growth in *propaganda*. This is both a business and a political phenomenon. It came into its own in the last war. Unhappily, there is no end in sight.

9. The advance in *mechanized warfare*. The curve has paralleled that of technology, with a crescendo in the bombing plane. The only hopeful thing about it is that war may become so dreadful that civilians may someday forego national sovereignty and embrace the world state.

10. The growing domination of *central governments*. The trend came in with the last war, has persisted for a genera-

tion, and seems to be riding into the future with unimpaired gusto.

11. The advance of *autarchy*. It began in the early 1920's, and there is no immediate end in sight. Every new synthetic abets it.

Our inventory is taken. You may question items or insist that others have been neglected. I have done the best I can according to my lights. I have tried to outline the trends that have come strongly to the fore since our promenade down State Street in the Spring of 1913. Some were implicit in the social structure then, some came in with the war, some with the depression. They are all found in America, but they are by no means confined to America. Every nation has been touched, if not moulded, by their impact. They help to make clear why Mussolini captured the imagination of the Italians, why Hitler became the strong man of Germany, why Chamberlain missed the bus, why Roosevelt got a third term. Above all, they make it clear that whoever wins the war, the great transition will go on.

History does not turn somersaults. There is always a reason for the path it takes. I have tried to show some of the reasons. These are the curves we have been riding, and if our judgment is cool we will look for an extension. Certain trends we cannot fail to ride for a long time to come, others may end their course more briefly. We have here a base for the exploration of the future. Whether it is a good future or bad, it is not my function to say. Some may welcome the vista, some may greatly fear it; but none should shut his eyes.

GOALS FOR AMERICA

BEFORE AN ARCHITECT or a statesman or anyone else can draw an intelligent plan, he must make an analysis of the goal he seeks. Before discussing economic plans for the postwar period, let us analyze in a general way some purposes which the plan should accomplish. The United States is a democratic country, and first of its goals should be to satisfy the needs and desires of the common people. These needs and desires cannot be measured in tons or miles or even dollars; they are expressed only indirectly in elections. They can be described, and the description will be a series of inferences. Here is my description of certain needs and desires, some of them nationwide, others worldwide. I am deeply convinced of their reality and power.

If you hold your ear close to the ground, you can hear a muffled roar echoing around the whole world. It does not come from bombs, or thunder on the Russian front. It is the voice of the people demanding security and an end to the paradox of plenty. It is the revolt of the masses asking for the food which farmers let rot upon the ground or dump into the streams. This subterranean roar is the most powerful force in the world today. Statesmen who listen to it will be upheld.

Statesmen who shut their ears will be buried, no matter how lofty their sentiments about freedom and initiative.

Science and invention have put an adequate standard of living within the reach of every family in the great industrial nations. Ultimately it will be within the reach of every family in the world. The mass of the people know this. Yet the standard of living which they might have does not come through to the great majority of them. Why does it not come through? It is there for all to see—13 million bales of cotton in storage, 500 million bushels of wheat in granaries in the United States, 60 million bags of coffee burned in Brazil—why does it not come through? The authorities reply that the market cannot tolerate it, or that the laws of property forbid it. Do you think these answers, however legal and logical, are going to satisfy the masses? They are asking a revolutionary question which demands a revolutionary answer.

We Want Security

The desire for security is displacing the desire to make a million. A generation ago, young men on State Street dreamed of becoming rich. Ask the next young college graduate you meet what he wants from life. The younger generation is turning away from the old goals and seeking new.

This profound and revolutionary urge for security, work and hope, affects all classes in the community, especially the middle income groups. The Townsend Old-Age Plan, before which Congressmen shiver, is primarily a middle class movement. The cult of the proletariat is engulfed in this wider mass demand. Indeed modern technology, by taking physical work away from hornyhanded toilers and giving it to machines, is destined to make the proletariat obsolete. The revolution is wider and deeper than anything Karl Marx imagined. Communism and socialism were the products of a strongly entrenched capitalistic society. When capitalism wanes, communism loses its traditional enemy, and it wanes with the power which gave it being. Who are the "bosses" when the United States Army takes over aircraft plants?

What is it the people want? They do not want words.

They want work: first, any kind of work in preference to unemployment; then, work which interests them. Man is a working animal, as any biologist will tell you.

They want to *belong:* to feel that they are part of a living community, that they have a place in it which other people recognize. The factory system has uprooted a deep-lying desire which found expression in handicraft communities. I do not speak without authority here. Fifteen years of research in the Hawthorne plant of the Western Electric Company fully confirm this statement.[23]

They want to be rid of worry about where the next meal is coming from, whether the rent can be paid, whether the wife can go to the hospital for the new baby, whether illness or old age is going to leave one an object of scorn and icy charity.

They want the things which quantity production has made so visible—an automobile, a radio or washing machine, silk stockings, a fur coat, a bathroom, tickets to the movies, a ball game, a concert, a vacation at the beach, a well-built house to live in, a high school education for the children, perhaps college for Harry who is forever reading books.

They want to be able to pick their things, their homes, their jobs.

23. See my article in the February 1941 *Reader's Digest:* "What Makes the Worker Like to Work?"

They do not want to be pushed around.

The above, I think, is applicable to all people, everywhere, who have come into contact with modern civilization. In the democratic nations we can list two additional desires:

People want to elect the men who govern them, and to have the right to depose them if they are not meeting popular demands.

People want to say what they please without a secret service agent around every corner. In Britain and America the Bill of Rights is almost as universal as the air they breathe. In the totalitarian countries this desire is muted. Ultimately it may become world-wide.

Hitler's Social Challenge

The list of wants falls into two main divisions. First, we note the economic desires—a job, social security, adequate living standards. Second, we note psychological desires—hope for the future, a sense of being a part of the community, of belonging. Sometimes, as the Western Electric studies show, this desire is stronger than that for higher wages, shorter hours or better working conditions.

The National Socialism of Germany gave at first some scope to both these basic wants. Hitler provided employment, opportunity and hope to the young people of the Reich. He promises peace, security and a New Order in Europe. On the other hand, his Gestapo cruelly pushes people around, and he allows no votes, no Bill of Rights.

The democratic countries have taken their voting and freedom of speech for granted, and until recently their governments have given no expression to the economic demand for work and security, and very little expression to the desire for hope, and for the sense of belonging to the community. Julian Huxley has put the case thus:[24] The democracy of Britain, he says, has fallen down on three counts. It has done nothing about insecurity, with its consequent fear and anxiety. Unemployment has been the visible sign of this failure. It has done nothing to stimulate the feeling of group solidarity, of cohesion in the community as a whole. People have lacked a deep sense of purpose in life. Thirdly, it has done nothing to break down the class system, with its glaring inequalities of power, wealth and prestige. The first two indictments apply equally to the United States; the third not so much. Our old school ties are fortunately not so strong as in Britain. We are a pioneering people, and most of us do not bow down to lords and gentlemen.

The challenge to the democracies is not so much a military one, in the long run, as it is a social one. Can the democracies provide the goods which the people demand in this revolutionary age, and continue to be democracies? It will be useless to beat Hitler in war, and not provide the goods. More Hitlers will arise, more Mussolinis, Stalins, Huey Longs, Francos, until the demands of the people are met.

The United States has everything it takes to meet the challenge except recognizing that there is one. It has the resources, the man power, the science and the technical skills, to give the people all they demand, without surrendering the ballot or the Bill of Rights. But many leaders think it demoralizing to give people what they want; others think that the country cannot find the money for it; others do not want to be bothered with thinking about it at all.

In 1940, 80 million Americans lived in families where the

24. *Democracy Marches*, Chatto and Windus, 1941.

income was less than $1,500 a year. Forty-five millions were living below the diet danger line. Twenty millions were living on an average of five cents a meal. The army allows forty-three cents a day, and the navy forty-six cents. If everyone in the United States ate at least as well as those living in families whose income was $1,200, the resulting demand for food would plow an area the size of Iowa, and add $2,000,000,000 to farmers' budgets. Hazel K. Stiebeling, an outstanding expert on nutrition, says that the country to keep healthy should consume 20 per cent more milk, 15 per cent more butter, 70 per cent more oranges, grapefruit and tomatoes, 100 per cent more green vegetables, 35 per cent more eggs. In depression years milk was poured into rivers, oranges and vegetables left on the ground to rot by the millions of tons.

More than 40 per cent of all young men drafted for the army have been rejected for poor health. The British recently took 1,000 young men so rejected, put them in a special camp, and gave them good, nourishing food for six months. They were then reexamined by the medical authorities, and 800 of them promptly passed the army tests!

Meanwhile, during the stagnation of the 1930's, it has been conservatively estimated that 100 million man-years of labor in this country were wasted through unemployment, and the National Resources Planning Committee calculates that, as a result, two hundred billion dollars' worth of potential goods and services were lost—the equivalent of a $6,000 house for every family in the country, or enough to build the railroad system of the nation five times over. No better illustration could be given of the paradox of plenty, that insane condition to which the mass of the people so reasonably object. As long as it continues, the dictators do not need to worry very much.

They can do better on the economic front without half trying.

What We Must Do

The idea of basic living standards is gaining momentum. Sometimes they are called "national minimums." One hears the demand from church groups, government officials, labor leaders, economists, scientists, even businessmen. It is perhaps heard louder in Britain than it is here. We have had public schools for many years. It is now proposed to add food, housing, medical care, clothing, to universal education. In this light, the proposal is not revolutionary in kind but only in scope. Instead of *one* essential guaranteed to the last child, we have *five* essentials guaranteed to the last family. Let us sample a few recent statements.

RUSSELL DAVENPORT, editor of *Fortune:*[25] "We demand an economic system that will yield every man, woman and child reasonable economic security against want and poverty, and reasonable economic opportunity for advancement, the development of talents, education, expansion and adventure. There is a minimum, not of subsistence, but of decency, at which every member of a modern state has a claim to economic protection. If we are to build a true democracy, this claim must be accepted as a fundamental economic right."

FORTUNE, unsigned article:[26] "A new doctrine is gaining ground: that nutrition is no less a right of the citizen than is education." School lunches to six million children, and the Food Stamp Plan, give evidence of this doctrine.

W. L. BATT, head of the SKF industries:[27] "I sincerely believe that if we tackle this problem of postwar demobilization

25. *Fortune,* August 1941.   26. August 1941.
27. Speech reported in *The New York Times,* December 4, 1940.

... with all the energy we are now devoting to the opposite process, we can build a standard of living the like of which the world has never dreamed. We can lay the groundwork for an industrial system that will have as its only limits the available man-power for production." Observe that Mr. Batt is not concerned with *financial* limits to production, but only with *physical* ones.

MAYOR LA GUARDIA of New York:[28] "Don't talk to me about surpluses. There is no such thing as surplus until every family in the country is properly housed, and every man, woman and child is properly fed and properly clad."

LEONARD K. ELMHIRST:[29] "The one possible base line for postwar planning is the need of all humanity for a minimum standard of life and living. . . . The simple idea is that no man, woman or child in the lowest income groups need suffer hunger, penury or degradation through causes beyond the control of the individual or the family."

THE NATIONAL RESOURCES PLANNING BOARD:[30] "We must plan to enable every human being within our boundaries to realize progressively the promise of American life in food, shelter, clothing, medical care, education, work, rest, home life, opportunity to advance, adventure, and the basic freedoms." That word "adventure" makes one wonder if the Planning Board had been reading *Fortune*. Russell Davenport used it too, and his magazine came out first. It is a good word in any living standard.

GROUP MEETING OF THE NATIONAL PLANNING ASSOCIATION:[31] "After the war the consumer must be regarded not as

28. Speech reported in *The New York Times*, August 21, 1941.
29. Article in *The Land*, Spring of 1941.
30. Pamphlet, August 1941, *After Defense—What?*
31. In New York, July 22, 1941.

the man who can buy but as the man who eats." The more you study this simple sentence the more devastating it becomes. Here is another from the same source: "Wheat has been viewed out of its context in the international situation as something which had to be bought, not as something which needed to be eaten, and which might be traded directly for other products." There is a whole new philosophy of foreign trade in this.

THE LONDON ECONOMIST:[32] "Yet the view is spreading that the time has come for the State to guarantee to every individual—as it has never done explicitly in peace—a sufficient quantity of food, clothing and shelter and the acknowledged necessities of life."

J. B. PRIESTLEY:[33] "There should be established—and we could do it now, and may have to do it soon—a basic minimum standard of living for every man, woman and child in the community. This applies to food, housing, clothing, health and education. The maintenance of this minimum should be the first charge upon the resources of the community, and while there are still people below it, there should be nobody above it. This is absolutely essential."

A BRITISH POLITICIAN, reported by Edward R. Murrow:[34] "The times call for great victories or great measures. There seems to be no possibility of great victories in the immediate future, so we must do something about the measures: we must promise security and equality after the war to the people who work with their hands, and make them believe we mean it. . . . This matter of social and economic reform will become more urgent as the war goes on." To which Mr. Murrow

32. July 6, 1940.   33. *Out of the People,* Harper, 1941.
34. In his broadcast from London, August 27, 1941.

adds: "You can't talk to workers in this country [Britain] without getting the impression that it's the little concrete everyday things that matter. Security, food, a decent home. They don't care much about the rest of the world if these things are provided."

FRANKLIN D. ROOSEVELT AND WINSTON CHURCHILL:[35] [We] "desire to bring about the fullest collaboration between all nations, in the economic field with the object of securing, for all, improved labor standards, economic adjustment and social security." This is high authority for the goal of universal security.

A Postwar Platform

In this parade of advocates for basic living standards, many functions are mentioned or clearly implied, which can be summarized in the following specific categories:

Full employment. All men and women seeking work which cannot be found in private industry should be employed by the state. If citizens are going to be guaranteed minimum standards on the one hand, they must help provide those standards by their labor on the other. Congenital loafers may be cared for in sanatoriums.

Full and prudent use of material resources. Idle plant and idle machines must become as great a scandal as idle men. Natural resources, however, especially soils, waters, forests, must be utilized without progressive deterioration of these assets. The resource budget must be balanced, and our national heritage maintained. Minerals are by their nature wasting assets, but they must be exploited thriftily, with constant research devoted to substitutes.

35. In their Eight Point Program, signed at sea, August 14, 1941.

Guarantee of the five essentials to every citizen—food, housing, clothing, health services, education. The food standard should be on the basis of adequate nutrition, including the essential vitamins, not on the basis of calories alone. This is particularly important for growing children.

Social insurance at all major exposed points in the social structure. This would include old-age allowances, benefits for sickness, accident, temporary unemployment, childbearing. It is interesting to note that the Australian government, despite its heavy war commitments, has just voted an allowance for every child in the country where the family has more than one.

Labor standards. These would include minimum wages, maximum hours, standards for working conditions, in every branch of employment. The Wages and Hours Law of 1938 is a long step in this direction.

Where's the money coming from? Out of that one hundred million man-years of work wasted; out of that two hundred billion dollars of production which never was produced. It will come from the same place that the bombers, tanks and battleships are now coming from—out of the full employment of the people.

4

BACK TO BUSINESS AS USUAL?

I<small>T IS CLEAR</small> that the fulfill-
ment of the goals set forth in the last section is incompatible
with a program of business as usual. If business as usual be
defined as a condition where prices are set in the open market,
where hope of profit is the mainspring of new investment,
and where government acts only as umpire for a system of
free enterprise, one must go back to 1913 to find even an ap-
proximation of that structure. If the world could not retreat
to free enterprise after the last war—when the victors strongly
desired to—is there any hope that retreat will be possible
after this war? On the basis of the twenty-five year record,
there appears to be none.

Why can we not recapture a system which proved itself to
be a good system, and which most of our leaders, in Britain
and America at least, still prefer? Because the basic conditions which made it a good and workable system for a century
and more, have so changed that it has now become unworkable over great areas. Everybody admits that business as usual
will not work in wartime. The record shows that it will not
work in a time of deep depression, and further, that a system
which falls into such catastrophic depressions as that of 1929

is more than any community can long tolerate. The record shows that the *natural* culmination of the system is a series of giant corporations and cartels which are in effect a denial of the system. Not even Mr. Thurman Arnold and his blitzkrieg corps of bright young lawyers can pulverize these half-socialized monsters into small competing units. Not gain, but loss, would follow the breaking up of the American Telephone and Telegraph Company into small competing enterprises.

In war and peace, boom and depression, the march toward centralized, collective controls has continued. Planning has often been identified with socialism. Yet orthodox socialists themselves are far from pleased with the collectivism practiced in Russia, Germany, Italy, Japan, Spain, and they look with grave suspicion on the New Deal. Something has appeared which nobody anticipated, nobody wanted and nobody really understands. Mr. James Burnham has called it the "managerial revolution," in the first intelligent attempt to understand it which I have seen. Many more studies will be needed before the mystery is cleared up. We have something called "X," which is displacing the system of free enterprise, all over the world. If we do not know yet what to call it, we can at least describe its major characteristics. They include, in most countries:

Free Enterprise into "X"

A strong, centralized government.

An executive arm growing at the expense of the legislative and judicial arms. In some countries, power is consolidated in a dictator, issuing decrees.

The control of banking, credit and security exchanges by the government.

The underwriting of employment by the government, either through armaments or public works.

The underwriting of social security by the government—old-age pensions, mothers' pensions, unemployment insurance, and the like.

The underwriting of food, housing and medical care, by the government. The United States is already experimenting with providing these essentials. Other nations are far along the road.

The use of the deficit spending technique to finance these underwritings. The annually balanced budget has lost its old-time sanctity.

The abandonment of gold in favor of managed currencies.

The control of foreign trade by the government, with increasing emphasis on bilateral agreements and barter deals.

The control of natural resources, with increasing emphasis on self-sufficiency.

The control of energy sources—hydroelectric power, coal, petroleum, natural gas.

The control of transportation—railway, highway, airway, waterway.

The control of agricultural production.

The control of labor organizations, often to the point of prohibiting strikes.

The enlistment of young men and women in youth corps devoted to health, discipline, community service and ideologies consistent with those of the authorities. The CCC camps have just inaugurated military drill.

Heavy taxation, with especial emphasis on the estates and incomes of the rich.

Not much "taking over" of property or industries in the old socialistic sense. The formula appears to be *control without ownership*. It is interesting to recall that the same formula is used by the management of great corporations in depriving stockholders of power.

The state control of communications and propaganda.

These characteristics are incipient in some countries, full-blown in others. If you check off those which are observable in the United States in 1942; in Britain, in Germany, in Mexico, in Japan, in Sweden, in Russia, a comparison of check-marks will show some amazing parallels. Is the whole list good or bad? That is a meaningless question. Some items point strongly to community survival, which is perhaps the most fundamental good there is. Some are clearly contrary to the liberal democratic ideal. Most of them are anathema to the doctrines of Adam Smith. Good or bad, there they are, in the middle of the stage.

Study this list and think hard about it. At first reading, most Americans will not recognize it as something which applies to them. Yet there is not an item on the list which is not applicable in some degree to the United States. We have no official propaganda bureau yet, but the FCC controls radio broadcasting. Further, it is not a war list, though the war has increased the impact. These items are referents for "X," the new structure which is being molded, and for which there is as yet no name. Names are thrown around—"socialism," "state capitalism," "fascism,"—but they mean nothing, and only lead to confusion.

Can the list be modified when the war ends? Let us take a little testimony.

New Era Advocates

MAYOR LA GUARDIA, in the speech quoted above on goals for America, comes out flatly for a new order after the war. Otherwise the economic system faces complete collapse in the demobilization period. "It is going to be an American order, suited to our country and our way of life. . . . The cost of this readjustment . . . is going to be just as great for a few years as the cost of the national defense program." Not much hope for business as usual in the Mayor's horoscope.

HERBERT FEIS, of the State Department:[36] "This country is not likely to reconcile itself to the conclusion that full employment for all and the full use of our resources is only possible when conditions of war or needs of defense make it possible." It does not take a very high IQ to ask why we cannot keep prosperous making plowshares if it has been proved that we can keep prosperous making swords.

WALTER REUTHER, labor leader:[37] "We cannot fight this war and go back to 1933."

BUSINESS WEEK:[38] "It is inconceivable that when the defense program ends . . . the government will stand idly by in the midst of a great unemployment crisis born of nationwide demobilization. . . . The operation of the profit motive will be limited by the dominant requirement of full employment for the people." *Business Week* is telling corporation executives what to get ready for. Citizens, it says, are bound to ask "If war can turn wheels, why can't peace?"

PHILIP D. REED, Chairman of the Board, General Electric Company:[39] "Our political, social and economic scheme of things after the war will resemble neither the 1920's nor the 1930's. The war will advance by several decades the trends away from laissez-faire and toward economic planning under government supervision." Mr. Reed, it appears, has been studying trends.

E. R. STETTINIUS, U. S. Steel Corporation:[39] "The goal of production shall not be profit alone. This is the spirit of our age." Another trend follower.

36. *The Changing Pattern of International Economic Affairs.* Harper, 1940.
37. Quoted in *Fortune,* August 1941.
38. Issue of August 16, 1941.
39. *Business Week,* issue of August 16, 1941.

W. L. BATT, of the WPB: "We must face the perfectly plain, inescapable and inevitable fact that when this war is over, no matter who wins, the world will not resemble the world of 1939. . . . I want to go on record right here with the assertion that capitalistic imperialism and individual control of great financial and economic power is as dead in England today as the feudal system." The United States, Mr. Batt goes on to say, is only a step behind England in the transition. This is a high-powered businessman talking, not Norman Thomas.

We Can't Go Back

Despite the trend curves and the statements of business-men quoted above, there may be a very considerable popular ground swell when the war ends in favor of scrapping everything and going back to the good old days. It will not make sense, but it may have to be faced. Many people, espe-cially older people, will be weary to death of taxes, priorities, armaments, government decrees, forced savings, lease-lend-ing around the globe. They will have borne it for patriotic motives, but now they will bear it no longer. They feel strong-ly that the government must be thrown out of business, and that the United States must be thrown out of world affairs. They are sick of the whole bloody show. Something like this appeared after Versailles, in 1920.

This feeling will probably come again. But the brute facts this time promise to give it little scope in tangible action. Look at these figures. The National Resources Planning Board has given us a conservative preview of the situation when the war ends.[40]

40. *After Defense—What?,* pamphlet published August 1941, before U. S. entered war.

	In 1941	In 1944
Man power in military service	1,800,000	3,500,000
Man power in defense industries	4,800,000	23,500,000
Total in war work	6,600,000	27,000,000
Man power in peace industries	45,200,000	33,000,000
Man power unemployed	5,100,000[41]	0
Total man power	56,900,000	60,000,000

If these vast military outlays stop in 1944, there will be twenty-seven million Americans looking for work; three million odd from the army, full of energy and potential wrath. If there is any way by which business as usual can handle this explosive situation, then I have wasted a lifetime studying business practices. Of course, the twenty-seven million will not be demobilized overnight, and an inconclusive peace might require continuance of a larger military machine than after the last war, but the end might come with appalling rapidity, following, say, a complete defeat of the Axis, or a negotiated peace with the officers of a German army which had eliminated Hitler.

Program for Action

The Resources Board estimates that the national income will reach $105,000,000,000 by 1944. Can we let it drop to sixty or seventy billions because we cannot afford to be prosperous any more? "The American people will never stand for this. Sooner or later they will step in and refuse to let matters 'work themselves out'." *Fortune* quotes a college boy in this

41. A test check of the unemployed by the WPA in July 1941 showed 5,600,000. Close enough.

connection: "I don't mind fighting if it is necessary. But I don't want to spend two or three years in the army and then come out only to be told by an aged idiot that I can't have a job until the budget is balanced." There will be more than twenty million men from the army and the munitions industries feeling like that in 1944.

The Resources Board recommends that national income be held at one hundred billion dollars with full employment; that a forty-hour week prevail, with young people and old people freed from work; that a modified system of free enterprise be maintained, sustained at key points by government controls. Full employment will be insured by a system of public works in housing, conservation, power development, transport facilities. Every effort should be made to develop new products for the consumer industries.

This program can only be taken as a kind of opening gun. The most significant thing about it is that the Resources Board looks to a "mixed" economy in which private enterprise shares the field with public works and government controls. This ties in with our conception of "X" and the list of supporting characteristics given earlier. This is what we have been experiencing, only more of the same to come. With the end of the war, certain government controls can relax, but to maintain full employment, others may have to be stepped up. The investment will shift from howitzers to housing, but it must continue to be a planned investment.

Win, lose or draw, we can never return to the world of 1928, or even of 1939. This may alarm many Americans but it does not alarm me. The old world was not so perfect that a better one cannot be found. We have high goals before us which technology, if not folklore, can guarantee. We have trends to follow which do not cut us off too suddenly from what has gone before. Everything which will be in the post-war adjustment is here in embryo now. It is a question not of kind but of degree.

5

THE PROBLEMS WE SHALL FACE

THE WAR WILL END SOME DAY. The army, the munitions workers, the public at large, can be expected to raise an unscalable political barrier to mass unemployment. Statesmen who advocate a retreat to the stagnation of the 1930's, because prosperity can no longer be afforded, will be retired very rapidly to private practice. But statesmen who listen to the people are going to have serious problems to solve. Here are some of them:

1. *Employment problems.* Where are the demobilized army and defense workers going to get new jobs? How are they to be trained for them? Will dismissal allowances help? Can young people who are working go back to school, and old people step aside?

2. *Investment problems.* What varieties of public works must be inaugurated to maintain jobs for all? Housing, conservation, hospitals and medical care, highways, schools, come to mind. Where are these investments to be located, and who is to operate them? How far can investment in private enterprise be expanded? What new products can be developed?

3. *Excess capacity problems.* The RFC has already put

some six billion dollars into new plants, while private capital is pouring out large sums to expand capacity for steel, aluminum, power generation, airplanes, ships. How is this capacity to be kept busy when war spending levels off? Who is going to own and operate the plants which the government is financing, or building outright? How can war contracts be liquidated gradually with aid to contractors while they find peacetime contracts? What happens to the older plants when war ends? What happens to the price of aluminum if the demand for airplanes drops 80 per cent?

4. *Financial problems.* How about the federal debt—will it be 200 billion dollars, as some now prophesy? How about taxation, the interest rate, the budget? How long must price controls and priorities be continued after the war ends? How are we going to finance those goals which the mass of the people demand, and which technology can guarantee as *physically* achievable? We shall have the man power, plant and natural resources; where are we going to find the money? It never can be found in the practices of traditional finance.

5. *Monetary problems.* What are we going to do with all that gold in Kentucky? If it proves to be useless as a monetary base, what other base can be substituted? Do we need a base at all? Germany seems to get along without one. Will money become primarily a bookkeeping device to move goods?

6. *Foreign trade problems.* Already American foreign trade has been completely distorted by depression and war. When peace comes, it will be unrecognizable. The war is making us more self-sufficient day by

day, cutting down the longtime need for imports. Nylon, synthetic rubber, plastics, aluminum from native clays—what will the crisis not bring? Fewer imports mean fewer exports; either that or another huge gift for suffering humanity beyond the seas. Of course we can give our goods away in the future with the same generosity which we have shown since 1917—about forty billion dollars' worth of goods have been handed out to date—but that hardly comes under the head of trade. It comes under the head of World Relief. A lot more relief may be necessary when the war ends, but sooner or later some program of orderly exchange must be inaugurated. We cannot go on subsidizing Europe, Asia and Africa indefinitely. A revival of the nineteenth century world free market is nowhere visible on our trend curves. What will the alternative be?

7. *Agricultural problems.* Government is deep in agricultural production and marketing today. After the war, markets for farm products abroad may be nonexistent. Subsidies for nonexistent markets make no sense. Yet there is a huge demand for more to eat in this country, as Hazel Stiebeling has demonstrated. How are we to substitute the domestic market for the foreign one, conserve our soils, eliminate rural slums?

8. *Political problems.* What changes in our political institutions will be necessary to make democracy more efficient, and more capable of swiftly meeting the great economic decision which government must make in the years before us? The threat of competition in efficiency by the totalitarian states may hang over us for a long time. Muddling through will not be good enough.

These and kindred problems we propose to explore in a series of books to follow this one. Here we have tried to indicate a trend. In the studies to come, we shall try to project the curves into the future.